PRESERVING MODERN LANDSCAPE ARCHITECTURE II
MAKING POSTWAR LANDSCAPES VISIBLE

edited by CHARLES A. BIRNBAUM, FASLA
with JANE BROWN GILLETTE and NANCY SLADE

sponsors
THE CULTURAL LANDSCAPE FOUNDATION
NATIONAL PARK SERVICE HISTORIC LANDSCAPE INITIATIVE
THE CATALOG OF LANDSCAPE RECORDS IN THE UNITED STATES AT WAVE HILL

with support from
FURTHERMORE: A PROGRAM OF THE J. M. KAPLAN FUND
THE GRAHAM FOUNDATION FOR ADVANCED STUDIES IN THE FINE ARTS
JONES & JONES ARCHITECTS, LANDSCAPE ARCHITECTS, LTD.
THE CULTURAL LANDSCAPE FOUNDATION

2004

PUBLISHER
Spacemaker Press, LLC
James G. Trulove, Publisher
1250 28th Street, NW
Washington, DC 20007
202-337-1380

DESIGN
James Pittman

ISBN 0-9749632-0-8

Printed in Korea

First printing, 2004

1 2 3 4 5 6 7 8 9 / 07 06 05 04

FRONT COVER
Cover photograph of the Miller
Garden, Columbus, Indiana, by
James Sheldon (courtesy of The
Cultural Landscape Foundation)

ACKNOWLEDGMENTS

Preserving Modern Landscape
Architecture II: Making Post War
Landscapes Visible, the follow-up to the
1995 Conference dedicated to the same
topic, was held at Wave Hill and
Columbia University in New York City
on April 5–6, 2002. The conference was
sponsored by The National Park Service
Historic Landscape Initiative, The CAT-
ALOG of Landscape Records in the
United States at Wave Hill, The Cultural
Landscape Foundation, The New York
Landmarks Conservancy, and Columbia
University Graduate School of
Architecture and Planning. The two-day
conference was designed to build on
the discourse begun seven years earlier
at Wave Hill.

The first day, held at Wave Hill,
focused on both promoting and celebrating recent advancements in the
preservation and management of modern landscape architecture. Speakers
from the United States, Canada,
Portugal, and the United Kingdom collectively addressed common challenges
and successful stewardship strategies.

The second day of the conference,
held at Columbia University, aimed at
initiating the development for a historic context to deal with modern
landscape heritage in New York City,
and beyond. The papers from this day
spotlighted the shapers of these often
"invisible" landscapes, aiming to
increase public support and wider
appreciation. Presentations celebrated
the legacies of Hideo Sasaki, Robert
Zion, and M. Paul Friedberg. Noted
historians Marc Trieb and Richard
Longstreth along with internationally
recognized landscape architects M.
Paul Friedberg, Stuart Dawson, Grant
Jones, and Laurie Olin also participated, providing the vivid and essential
historical context—from the perspective of both historians and participants.

In all, there were seventeen papers
delivered at the conference. This publication includes sixteen of those
papers, in many cases revised and
expanded. In addition, "Preserving the
Designed Landscape," a paper by
Lawrence Halprin has been added.

The essays conclude with a call to
action, the Wave Hill Charter, which
was signed by most attendees, who
were of the opinion that the time has
come for the American Society of
Landscape Architects (ASLA) to develop national guidance regarding the
preservation and management of modern landscape architecture. This
charter earnestly requests that the
ASLA develop a stewardship ethos for
addressing the documentation, treatment, and management of the modern
landscape legacy.

Many individuals contributed to the
conference and this publication. First,
we are most grateful to Catha Grace
Rambusch and Chris Panos at the CAT-
ALOG of Landscape Records in the
United States at Wave Hill. This is our
sixth conference collaboration; both
Catha and Chris, as always, provided
organizational wizardry and business
acumen. Thanks also to Roger Lang, at
the New York Landmarks Conservancy,
who assisted step-by-step and whose
participation allowed us to expand both
the audience and dialogue.

In making this publication a reality,
Jane Brown Gillette, Catha Rambusch,
and Nancy Slade have all provided
invaluable support as readers and co-
editors. In particular, Nancy Slade's
organizational support has been vital.
Thanks also to James Trulove and Peter
Walker at Spacemaker Press for supporting this project from the outset and to
James Trulove and designer James
Pittman for bringing it to completion.

This Publication could not have been
realized without the generous support
of Furthermore: a program of the J. M.
Kaplan Fund, The Cultural Landscape
Foundation, The Graham Foundation
for Advanced Studies in the Fine Arts,
Jones and Jones Architects, Landscape
Architects, LTD., ERA Architects, Inc.,
Storrow Kinsella Associates, Inc., and
Zion Breen & Richardson Associates.

It is our hope that the essays herein
continue to expand this discourse, that
they will provide vital inspiration and
context for educated decision making.
Peter Walker recently stated in Land
Forum (No 4, 1999), "The ideal solution
is to wait until the garden is sufficiently
mature to show its advantage-and then
publish the project at intervals for years
and years. We could then appreciate the
role of change in landscape architecture, and we could also see that time
changes more than landscape. It trans-
forms the human eye as well." May this
publication promote thoughtful stewardship practices, ones that will insure
healthy maturation of modern landscapes so that they will be understood
and enjoyed by future generations.

B 214 9219

CONTENTS

6   MOVING BEYOND THE PICTURESQUE
    AND MAKING POSTWAR LANDSCAPE
    ARCHITECTURE VISIBLE
    Charles A. Birnbaum

16 PRESERVE SOME, YES, BUT ALSO IMPROVE,
    ADD TO, AND LET SOME GO
    Laurie Olin

24 MODERN LANDSCAPE AT RISK
    Stuart O. Dawson

26 THEN AND NOW
    M. Paul Friedberg

32 SOCIAL FORCE: THE URBAN OPTIMISM OF
    M. PAUL FRIEDBERG
    Paul Bennett

38 PRESERVING THE DESIGNED LANDSCAPE
    Lawrence Halprin

42 SKYLINE PARK: PRESERVATION ETHICS AND
    PUBLIC SPACE
    Mark W. Johnson

50 CASE STUDY: MANHATTAN SQUARE PARK,
    ROCHESTER, NEW YORK
    Ken Smith

56 CHURCH, ECKBO, HALPRIN, AND THE
    MODERN URBAN LANDSCAPE
    Marc Treib

66 PRESERVING MODERN ARCHITECTURE AND
    LANDSCAPE ARCHITECTURE IN COLUMBUS,
    INDIANA
    Meg Storrow and John Kinsella

70 DAN KILEY: PLANTING ON THE GRID
    Gregg Bleam

80 NEW PARKS FOR NEW YORK
    Donald Richardson

84 THE NATURE OF MODERNITY: PRINCIPLES FOR
    KEEPING HISTORIC LANDSCAPES ALIVE
    Grant R. Jones

88 DESIGNATING MODERN CULTURAL LANDSCAPES
    IN CANADA
    Michael McClelland

96 OBSERVATIONS ON A MODERNIST: SIR PETER
    SHEPHEARD
    Edward Bennis

110 THE ORIGIN OF THE PROFESSION OF LANDSCAPE
    ARCHITECTURE IN PORTUGAL DURING THE
    MODERN MOVEMENT
    Cristina Castel-Branco

118 THE LAST LANDSCAPE
    Richard Longstreth

126 THE WAVE HILL CHARTER

Pennsylvania Station is now being wrecked, but its loss can help us in the fight ahead to save other such landmarks. Nothing can be accomplished without public enthusiasm; to get public support, the public's imagination must be captured. Public ignorance of the true greatness of Penn Station was, more than any other factor, responsible for its destruction. Those who knew said too little about the architectural qualities of the building, the spaces it created, the materials and workmanship that went into it. The public was asked to save Penn Station, but we never convincingly told them why.

The bitter lesson for New York and for all communities is that the public is the most vital factor in preservation. Imaginative use of landmark buildings must first be communicated to the public, and its interest and enthusiasm aroused, if we are not to lose our heritage to indifference.

Robert Zion, FASLA
January 1965

It is our hope that this collection of papers will educate everyone about the extraordinary legacy of modern landscape architecture that exists in New York City and beyond and about the pioneering mavericks who helped shape the built environment for ourselves and future generations.

Charles A. Birnbaum, FASLA

In Memory of Dan Kiley, 1912–2004

Moving Beyond the Picturesque and Making Postwar Landscape Architecture Visible

Charles A. Birnbaum

It has been nearly four years since the publication of *Preserving Modern Landscape Architecture* (Spacemaker Press, 1999) and eight years since the Wave Hill conference convened on this topic, cosponsored by the CATALOG of Landscape Records in the United States and the National Park Service's Historic Landscape Initiative. At the 1995 event both design and historic preservation professionals bemoaned the lack of recognition and the loss of modern landscape architecture. In recent years we have seen the passing of modern-era luminaries: A.E. Bye, Garrett Eckbo, Robert Marvin, Hideo Sasaki, Richard Webel, and Robert Zion. None of their work, not a single landscape, is listed on the National Register of Historic Places to date.

There have been isolated bursts of good news. North Americans have witnessed the designation of several works of landscape architecture from the recent past. This includes the General Motors Technical Center in Warren, Michigan, with "Significance in Landscape Architecture, Transportation, Engineering, and Architecture," and the first National Historic Landmark (NHL) designation for landscape architecture, titled "Modernism in Architecture, Landscape Architecture, Design, and Art in Bartholomew County, Indiana, 1942–1965." Additionally, the Province of Ontario recognized the Queens Park Complex designed by Sasaki Strong Associates as "a significant landscape of cultural and heritage value"—a first for Canada. For detailed discussions of these developments, refer to "Preserving Modern Architecture and Landscape Architecture in Columbus, Indiana" by Meg Storrow and John Kinsella and Michael McClelland's "Designating Modern Cultural Landscapes in Canada." Collectively, these designations represent the first recognition for modern landscapes designed by such masters as Thomas Church, Dan Kiley, and Hideo Sasaki.

Although these recent designations show great promise, the recent demolition of Riis Houses Plaza in New York City (M. Paul Friedberg, 1966) and Christopher Columbus Waterfront Park in Boston (Sasaki and Associates, 1976) shows that potential NHL landscapes can be destroyed. Others remain vulnerable—due in large part to their lack of recognition and registration. What will be the future of New York City's modern landscape architecture legacy listed in Table 1 or such worthy NHL candidates as the Kaiser Center Roof Garden in Oakland and Mellon Plaza in Pittsburgh (Figures 1 and 2)?

As an individual trained in landscape architecture while practicing historic preservation, let me pose a question in this introductory essay from the perspective of someone with a foot in both camps. This perspective, which I will refer to as a nature-culture stewardship ethic, is one that attempts to integrate and safeguard historic and cultural resource values

Figure 1. The Kaiser Center Roof Garden in Oakland, designed by Ted Osmundson, was the first privately built—and, at the time, the largest—roof garden in the postwar era. Opened in 1960, the carefully maintained three-acre park sits atop a twenty-eight-story office tower. The project has inspired similar work internationally. Without question, the park is a NHL candidate. (Courtesy, Ted Osmundson)

Figure 2. Mellon Plaza was the first park ever constructed over a parking garage. The project was begun in 1948, completed in 1951. Simonds described the project as a "platform, a structure, an island, a space, a focal center, a civic monument, a gathering place, an oasis." Today the structures that surround the park are all listed on the National Register, yet the park, which perhaps has greater significance, has not been designated to date. (Courtesy, author)

within the design process. As a historic preservation professional I seldom "select" a period of significance. I look to research, inventory, and analysis, essentially part one of a cultural landscape report, to reveal, organize, articulate, and assess the multiple values and meanings that survive in the cultural landscape today. This is my design philosophy. This is my stewardship ethos.

In reading the papers included in this volume I suggest that we consider this nature-culture stewardship ethic for broader adoption by the landscape architecture and historic preservation professions alike. Within this context let us consider the stewardship patterns that have emerged. What distinguishes the approach of embracing a landscape's multiple layers from appreciating landscape designs with a single significant association? Unlike many postwar urban projects by Lawrence Halprin, Paul Friedberg, or Robert Zion, this introductory essay draws attention to the myriad historic preservation and design issues that may be found within a landscape's multiple layers.

Direction from the Profession's Leadership

Since the early 1970s landscape architects have learned to *Design with Nature*.[1] Today, leading design and planning professionals consider the inventory and analysis of environmental systems and natural resources as an integral part of the design and planning process. Why is it, then, that the same professionals have not gained an appreciation of how to Design with Culture?

A review of the 1993 Declaration on Environment and Development by the American Society of Landscape Architects (ASLA) suggests that the landscape architecture profession is unclear about its position on cultural landscapes. It states that "environmental and cultural integrity must be maintained even while sustaining human well-being and the level of development needed to achieve it." The declaration proceeds to define sustainable development as "development that meets the needs of the present without compromising the future."[2]

By comparison, if we review the ASLA Definition of Landscape Architecture that was adopted by the Board of Trustees in 1983, we find the statement that landscape architecture "is the profession which applies artistic and scientific principles to the research, planning, design, and management of both natural and built environments. Practitioners of this profession apply creative and technical skills and scientific, cultural, and political knowledge in the planned arrangement of natural and constructed elements on the land with a concern for the stewardship and conservation of natural, constructed, and human resources."[3]

As this statement shows, the profession's awareness for treating and managing cultural landscapes was on the increase in the early 1980s. Yet, as suggested by more recent policy statements, the profession has since diluted its primary focus and as a result has been slow to integrate preservation-planning principles into its present-day stewardship ethic.

It is within this context that three current controversies involving modern landscape architecture should be considered: Christopher Columbus Waterfront Park in Boston (Figure 3), the three-block Skyline Park in Denver, and the sunken sculpture courtyard at the Virginia Museum of Fine Arts in Richmond (Figure 4). The ASLA has been absent from any discourse about these three seminal works of landscape architecture, the first designed by Sasaki Associates, the second and third by Lawrence Halprin. In effect the ASLA has no opinion about these and other new development projects, all driven by use or economics, which will result in a loss or degradation of character-defining landscape features central to the original design intent. In the case of the three projects, outright demolition is anticipated or has already been accomplished. Where is the nature-culture ethic in this work?

The Profession of Landscape Architecture Today Among the more than 30,000 landscape architects practicing in the United States today, some 13,000 are members of the ASLA. About two hundred of these individuals actively participate as members of the society's Historic Preservation professional interest group or of the Alliance for Historic Landscape Preservation, an independent group. Hence, based on professional affiliations, only two percent of practicing landscape architects are actively interested in this topic, while a much larger percentage of the profession view it as "specialized."

Perhaps this mentality is fueling a schism: There are those who preserve—and there are those who design. It is to this psychological juncture that many find themselves relegated by family, friends, colleagues, the public, and the press. It is within this countercurrent that many are expected to don the hat of the preserver/advocate who stands in the way of progress and creativity, willing to lie down in front of the bulldozer. Conversely, the other perceived option is to assume the stereotype of the design professional who prescribes the necessary vision while possessing sufficient panache to convince others that they too may be among the chosen.

How did landscape architects come to this junction? Were others who came before our generation also labeled and marginalized? How did New England pioneers of the profession beginning with Frederick Law Olmsted, Robert Morris Copeland, and Charles Eliot with their interest in the preservation of scenery and historical sites identify,

Figure 3. Sasaki Associates designed Christopher Columbus Waterfront Park in the mid-1970s. This revolutionary design reclaimed Boston's harbor by commemorating its former industrial past. What could have been a formulaic urban-renewal project became instead one of America's earliest modern waterfront parks, one that established a national design standard. Opened during the Bicentennial celebrations, the park was destroyed in 2001. (Sasaki Associates)

Figure 4. Lawrence Halprin's 1976 design (with architects Hardwicke Associates) for the North Wing expansion of the Virginia Museum of Fine Arts is a sculpture garden as metaphor with a complex combination of sensory and visual experiences. As a focal point anchoring the garden layers to the ground plane, an extraordinary fountain simultaneously reinforces the symbiotic relationships between garden and building, landscape and art. The fountain's sculptural grouping of rectangular limestone blocks rising up from a shallow reflecting pool was precisely scaled to embrace Aristide Maillol's sculpture The River, purchased by the museum in 1970 in anticipation of eventual placement within the new outdoor space. Today, Halprin's sculpture garden has not been recognized for its historic significance, and as a result it is threatened with eradication. (Courtesy, author)

nurture, educate, and empower their constituency? Who were these often-referenced "leaders in village improvements, lovers of out-of-doors or of scenes associated with history or old times, leaders in horticulture or historical societies" whom Eliot rallied together to start this crusade in 1890?[4]

It was just seven years later that Eliot's obituary, appearing in *Garden & Forest*, noted that his "greatest public service was the organization of the Board of Trustees for the preservation of beautiful and historic places in Massachusetts."[5] Eliot biographer Keith Morgan suggests that his work "became a model for subsequent efforts such as the National Trust in Great Britain, and ultimately, the National Trust in the United States."[6] Where is this leadership a century later? Who will fill this void and build the essential bridges between landscape architecture and historic preservation? Why is it acceptable to disregard the work of those who came before us? Is it sufficient to celebrate a work upon completion and thereafter allow it to fade physically, through conscious management decisions or by its very absence from course materials for students of landscape architecture, history, and historic preservation?

Professional Practice and Palimpsests

This was not always the situation. If we look at the response by landscape architects to earlier design contributions in the first half of the twentieth century we can see a startling pattern of sympathetic change and continuity. Why did Fletcher Steele integrate Nathan Barrett's earlier work into his gracious and completely innovative vision at Naumkeag? Why didn't the Olmsted firm obliterate Barrett and Bogart's earlier and clearly more conventional work at Newark's Branch Brook Park? Why didn't Arthur Shurcliff plow under Olmsted's meandering watercourse at the Back Bay Fens? Instead, by refining its edge and creating a "lagoon," he was better able to integrate proposed park uses and unite the park with its adjacent neighbors, such as the Museum of Fine Arts. Even more recently, in 1977, at the Back Bay Fens, this understanding of the design continuum was extended when Carol Johnson's office developed a master plan complete with new pedestrian bridges. Ultimately, this plan was revisited by the Department of Environmental Management's Olmsted Historic Landscape Preservation Program in 1984, and a preservation master plan was published in 2001. The story goes on. As we can see at the Fens or at the Alice in Wonderland landscape surrounds, designed by Hideo Sasaki for Central Park, new work can stand on its own while being part of a symphonic common language.

What can we learn from these examples? How do they relate to our code of ethics as landscape architects and to the ways that we apply preservation-planning and treatment principles? Within this context, can we

Figure 5. The Camden Amphitheatre in Maine is noticeably absent from the Walker-Simo survey as well as from other books on modern landscapes. Designed by Fletcher Steele in 1929, it is conceivably the first public modernist garden in the United States. (Courtesy, author, photograph by Peter Hornbeck)

justify the destruction or alteration of historic designed landscapes in part or in total? If this "invisible" design legacy in all of its chronological manifestations goes unrecognized, unidentified, and undocumented, does it then remain vulnerable to alterations that compromise its authenticity and the significant design continuum?

Rediscovering the Legacy

In their book *Invisible Gardens: The Search for Modernism in the American Landscape* (1994) Peter Walker and Melanie Simo set out to make visible the work of American landscape architects since World War II, from 1945 to the late 1970s. The authors find in this period "one great surge of collective energies—the modern movement, an upheaval of traditional values, beliefs, and artistic forms that have evolved over centuries of the Western world." (The authors find limited evidence of this work before World War I, but within the discipline of landscape architecture, they note that the impact of the modern movement was "more gradual and often less striking than in other visual and spatial arts, yet no less profound.") Confirming this lack of recognition, Walker and Simo note that "reasoned criticism did not follow, and modern landscapes slipped beyond even the peripheral vision of art historians"[7] (Figures 5 and 6).

It is all too easy to lament the loss of modern landscape architecture—from New York City's pedestrian malls and plazas (for example, Paper Mill Plaza by Sasaki Associates, 1983) to urban playgrounds and plazas designed by M. Paul Friedberg (for example, Police Plaza, 1973). The goal of this introduction is, however, to provide a dual vision—with one eye on design and the other on history—or "rehabilitation," if we were to put this within the context of the *Secretary's Standards for Historic Preservation Projects*. To do this, I will consider two case studies, each of

Figure 6. Aerial view of Lake of the Isles and Lake Calhoun, Minneapolis, ca. 1920s (Courtesy, author)

Figure 7. Lake of the Isles with Eckbo-era additions and alterations (Birnbaum, 2000)

Figure 8. Pavilion in Minnehaha Park before "restoration" work: Note how the structure is subordinate and recedes in the landscape. (Birnbaum, 1994)

Figure 9. Pavilion in Minnehaha Park after "restoration" work, complete with off-the-shelf furnishings, features, and finishes (Birnbaum, 2000)

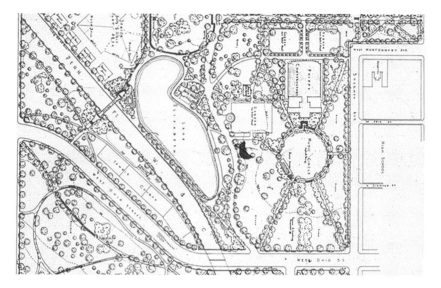

Figure 10. Development Plan for Northside Commons by Ralph Griswold, ca. 1930 (Northside Leadership Council)

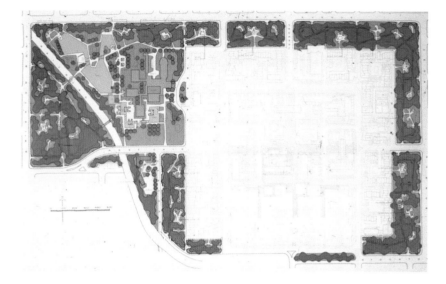

Figure 11: Proposed Long Range Development Plan for Allegheny Commons by Simonds and Simonds, April 1966 (Courtesy, author).

Figure 12. Edge of Lake Elizabeth with its reshaped trapezoidal configuration (Birnbaum, 2001)

Figure 13. Moving beyond the picturesque: The Civil War memorial is integrated with the reconfigured lake, bridges, and furnishings. (Birnbaum, 2001)

**Table 1: Modern Landscape Architecture in New York City:
Potential Candidates for Registration and Preservation**

Adventure Playground, Central Park	1967	Richard Dattner	Playground
Alice in Wonderland Node, Central Park	1960	Hideo Sasaki	Play Area
Ancient Play Garden	1972	Richard Dattner	Playground
Brooklyn Promenade	1958	Clarke & Rapuano	Promenade
Chase Manhattan Bank Plaza	1955–1961	Isamu Noguchi	Courtyard/Walled Garden
Co-op City	1971	Zion & Breen	Housing
Ford Foundation	1967	Dan Kiley	Courtyard/Interior Plaza
Greenacre Park	1971	Sasaki, Dawson & Demay	Vest-pocket Park
IBM Atrium	1983	Robert Zion	Courtyard/Interior Plaza
Lincoln Center, Damrosh Park	1959–1969	Dan Kiley Richard Webel	Plaza
Sculpture Court, Museum of Modern Art	1961–	Philip Johnson/ Zion & Breen	Courtyard/Walled Garden
Noguchi Museum Garden	1985	Isamu Noguchi/ Shogi Sazao, Architect	Sculpture Garden
Paley Park	1967	Zion & Breen	Vest-pocket Park
P.S. 166 Playground	1967	M. Paul Friedberg	Playground
Rockefeller University	1957	Dan Kiley	Campus
Stuyvesant Town	1947	Gilmore D. Clarke	Apartment Complex
Unisphere Plaza, World's Fair	1964	Gilmore D. Clarke	Plaza
United Nations North Garden	1947–1952	Gilmore D. Clarke	Plaza and Park
Washington Square Village	1959	Sasaki, Walker Associates	Housing/Walled Garden

Other Sites with Limited Integrity

Carver Houses	1964	M. Paul Friedberg	Housing Recreation Area
Central Park Entrances		Clark & Rapuano	Park Rehabilitation
Jacob Riis Houses Plaza	1966	M. Paul Friedberg	Housing Recreation Area
One Chase Manhattan Bank Plaza	1960/1972	SOM/Jean Dubuffet	Plaza Design with Group of Four Trees
Police Plaza	1973	M. Paul Friedberg	Plaza Design
77 Water Street	1970	Corchia-deHarak/A.E. Bye	Plaza Design
140 Broadway	1967	SOM/Isamu Noguchi	Plaza Design with The Red Cube
Hans Christian Andersen, Central Park	1956	Hideo Sasaki	Play Area

which represents more than a century of design, beginning with their initial conceptions by mid-to-late nineteenth-century landscape gardeners. Next, I will consider the ongoing stewardship of this original design intent by early twentieth-century landscape architects, followed by an examination of modern revisions to these collective works by seminal figures of the landscape architecture profession between 1967 and the early 1970s. Although both of these projects demonstrate the nature-culture stewardship advocated in this essay, the modern contributions are, ironically, still invisible and even misunderstood.

What is perhaps most compelling is that through recent project work, modern landscape features and embellishments once perceived as being outside the period of significance by preservation professionals—and even less attractive to the public and present-day stewards—are now taking their rightful place in the projects' historic continuua. Ironically, this criticized work would actually meet today's *Standards for Rehabilitation*.

Shared Vision: The Minneapolis Park System and the Lake of the Isles Growing rapidly in the last quarter of the nineteenth century, Minneapolis established a Park Board in 1883. Among its first acts was to hire landscape gardener H.W.S. Cleveland (1814–1900), who later that year would articulate his design intent in his *Suggestions for a System of Parks and Parkways, for the City of Minneapolis*. While Cleveland did not make specific recommendations for the entire system, his vision of scenic parkways and natural vistas guided the Park Board's work, including the development of water features that was closely followed by the system's first superintendent, William Morse Berry.[8]

Following the Cleveland/Berry tenure, Theodore Wirth served as superintendent of parks from 1906 to 1935 (and as superintendent emeritus until his death in 1950). His previous experience as superintendent of parks for ten years in Hartford, Connecticut, followed by three years working under Samuel Parsons at New York City's Parks Department, made him the ideal candidate for the rapidly growing system. Wirth came to Minneapolis after "some of the first acquisitions had been made, but little improvement work had been undertaken."[9] His work included designing many new parks, building out the system, acquiring new parkland, and even dredging the "formerly mosquito-infested, malaria-breeding swamps." In sum, he realized and expanded H.W.S. Cleveland's legacy. Immediately following Wirth's tenure, from the 1940s to the 1960s, little happened in the larger historic parks as the Park Board focused its attention on developing neighborhood parks.

In the 1970s Garrett Eckbo was hired to evaluate the Minneapolis park system. He concluded that the parkways surrounding the Lake of the Isles, the center link in the Chain of Lakes on the city's western edge, was overused. Eckbo's approach echoed H.W.S. Cleveland's original design intent, stated in his 1883 *Suggestions for a System of Parks and Parkways*, that "the beauties of nature" not be profaned "by the introduction of cheap decorations."[10] At Eckbo's recommendation, the parkways surrounding the lake were narrowed, traffic was made one-way, and parking bays were introduced. Other changes included the installation of a bike path, signage, and new furnishings including light standards, bollards, and benches. These changes to the parks and parkways during the 1970s minimally affected their integrity. Even today Eckbo's design vocabulary seems thoroughly modern, often low to the ground and outside of view, employing sympathetic colors and natural and translucent materials, all of which recede. The work aligns with the *Standards for Rehabilitation* in that the new work is distinguishable from the old and is of a compatible scale, proportion, and massing. Perhaps most important, historic spatial and visual relationships and significant circulation and water features retain their integrity unimpaired.

Compare this work performed outside a historic preservation framework with the work that was done most recently in the 1990s in Minnehaha Park under the guise of a historic preservation project. The new work alters or severs key spatial and visual relationships by "plunking" down new features such as fountains, pergolas, plazas, and statuary. It uses off-the-shelf Prairie-inspired lights and furnishings, which give "a false sense of history" and therefore do not even meet the *Standards for Restoration*. Perhaps most unfortunate, these new design solutions contradict Cleveland's own quest to avoid the "introduction of cheap decorations" and in all situations place an increased maintenance burden on the park. In sum, the new work fails as both sustainable landscape

architecture and historic preservation and brings to an end a century-long legacy of design continuity. The great irony is that it was Garrett Eckbo who stated in *Landscape for Living* that we should take "nothing for granted, accept no precedents without examination, and recognize a dynamic world in which nothing is permanent but change itself."[11]

Lost Language: Allegheny Commons, Pittsburgh, Pennsylvania

Allegheny Commons is the oldest mapped parkland in Pittsburgh and dates to the establishment of the Borough of Allegheny in 1783. It was not until 1867, however, that a Park Commission was appointed and the park laid out by William H. Grant (1815–1896) of Mitchell Grant & Co, New York City. Although little is known of the firm, the original park plan, when viewed in concert with contemporary research, can illuminate what was designed and actually built.[12]

The park's original design was to "be simple and have none of the pretensions to intricacy or labyrinthine composition so essential to the natural treatment of the grounds."[13] According to recent research, by the late 1860s "the lake had already been excavated, made water-tight, and filled." Historic photos show its "highly irregular perimeter contours, enhanced by plantings and at least one rockery, which almost gives the appearance of islands in water."[14] Although no comprehensive plan would be undertaken for the park until the mid-1930s, many of the original landscape features, including grand avenues, bridges, monuments, fountains, statuary, garden areas, and, perhaps most beloved, Lake Elizabeth, would change very little.

In 1935 a series of Existing Conditions surveys were prepared that provide an excellent record of the surviving Mitchell Grant period. Compared with the proposed Development Plans, they illustrate the extent of the new work and the continuity of design intent. A tennis court was added to an existing play area, garden beds were added to the Phipps Conservatory, an asphalt circle was turned into a Music Circle, and a play area for boys and girls was added to parkland at the heavily trafficked western corner. All of this work, executed by the City Planning Commission under landscape architect Ralph Griswold, superintendent of parks, does not alter any key spatial elements in the design.[15] In addition, many features such as Lake Elizabeth, the railroad right-of-way, West Ohio Street, and the majority of park walks remained the same.

In the following decade, during World War II, Lake Elizabeth was drained and used to store scrap metal. By the 1950s the Phipps Conservatory was in ruins, and the park was well on its way to a considerable state of decline. In 1966 a long-range development plan was undertaken to reverse this trend. Now thirty-five years later, there is once again a desire to undertake park master planning.

In 2000 the City's Northside Leadership Conference made a commitment for long-range planning for the Commons. In an attempt to offer guidance for this work I made my first trip to the park. During this visit and a subsequent walk later that spring, I learned that preservation professionals and community residents alike wanted to remove the trapezoidal-shaped lake that had been added at a later date. During these visits I asked who the designer of this water feature was. No one could tell me. It was, after all, John Simonds, the designer of Mellon Park, the first park built over a parking garage in the United States and the author of the classic 1961 text *Landscape Architecture*, which still serves as a standard reference today.

After making this discovery, I contacted Simonds. In our conversations and in a subsequent letter he stressed that "the two underlying objectives at that time were to convert the Commons into a more useable and safer open space and to [create] a focal point and stimulus to the revitalization of the lower north-side slum." Simonds himself stated that "it worked."[16]

Overall, in Simonds' plan, park-related land uses remained the same over time, and as in Eckbo's Minneapolis work, spatial and visual relationships were preserved and even reinforced. In sum, the work is respectful of the *Standards for Rehabilitation*, insuring that the alterations do not radically change, obscure, or destroy character-defining spatial organization, land patterns, or features. Throughout this project, new furnishings and light fixtures stand on their own, although they have not stood the test of time as successfully as those in the Minneapolis parks.[17]

Much of the work realized from the 1966 plan thoughtfully integrates the new with the old. It embodies the principles set forth in the epilogue to Simonds's first edition of *Landscape Architecture*, published five years earlier:

> The perception of relationships produces an experience. If the relationships are unpleasant, the experience is unpleasant. If the relationships sensed are those of fitness, convenience, and order, the experience is one of pleasure, and the degree of pleasure is dependent on the degree of fitness, convenience, and order. . . . *Fitness* implies the use of the right shape, the right size, and the right material. *Convenience* implies facility of movement,

lack of friction, comfort and reward. *Order* implies a logical sequence and a rational arrangement of parts.[18]

In November 2000 the firm of Pressley Associates was hired to prepare a report. At the time of this writing the community has come full circle and now embraces this modernist landscape feature, along with the preservation and restoration of its unique bridges, geometrical landforms, and plantings. To date they have not endorsed the preservation of the walls and lights from this later period, but I remain optimistic.

Simonds is one of Pittsburgh's native sons. It could be argued that Simonds's impact on the city's *cultural* landscape is no less significant than Andy Warhol's. Yet he has faded from memory and it took an outsider to rediscover this local landmark and engage its original designer in this discourse. How did this significant contribution fade to oblivion? What was it that made it any less desirable as a landscape experience than its picturesque precursor? Why had the earlier hand-tinted postcards from the 1910s—of families in their finery in rowboats or children splashing and wading—captured the attention and hearts of today's residents? Why couldn't they move beyond this romanticized version of the past?

As we can see from these two case studies, it is essential for the picturesque to coexist with the modern, allowing each distinct and historically significant contribution to stand on its own. This juxtaposition of elements that are both powerful and subtle can also teach visitors to celebrate unique regional expressions, accentuated by "authentic" nineteenth-century features alongside equally important "modern" postwar contributions. In summary, our challenge is to determine how we can get the general public as well as the professional design and historic preservation communities to understand and value this palimpsest, particularly given the current fad for easy-to-build, anonymous, no-brainer pastiche parks with Victorian-inspired benches, lights, and trash receptacles.

It is the aim of this collection of essays to initiate a discourse among the various allied disciplines to encourage them, as professionals, to take the necessary steps that would nurture greater public support and understanding for landscape architecture beyond the picturesque.

Charles A. Birnbaum, FASLA, is the coordinator of the National Park Service Historic Landscape Initiative, Washington, D.C. He edited Preserving Modern Landscape Architecture *(Spacemaker Press, 1999), which was the precursor to this publication.*

NOTES

1 Ian McHarg's *Design with Nature* was first published in 1968 by the Garden City Press, New York. Since then the book has been on almost every required reading list at undergraduate and graduate programs of landscape architecture.

2 The ASLA Declaration on Environment and Development and its Policies are stated on pages 42–45 of the 1999 edition of *The Members Handbook*. The declaration was adopted unanimously by the ASLA Board of Trustees in Chicago, October 1993.

3 1992 ASLA *Members Handbook*, p. 2.

4 Charles W. Eliot, *Charles Eliot, Landscape Architect* (Boston: Houghton Mifflin and Company, 1902). This letter is included in Appendix II, p. 752.

5 Obituary, *Garden and Forest*, 1897, p. 130.

6 Keith Morgan, "Charles Eliot" in Charles Birnbaum and Julie K. Fix, eds., *Pioneers of American Landscape Design II: An Annotated Bibliography* (Washington, D.C.: U.S. Department of the Interior, National Park Service, Historic Landscape Initiative, 1995), pp. 47–49.

7 Peter Walker and Melanie Simo, *Invisible Gardens: The Search for Modernism in the American Landscape* (Cambridge: The MIT Press, 1994), p. 3. Along with *Landscape Architecture: A Critical Review*, edited by Marc Treib (Cambridge: The MIT Press, 1993), sufficient context exists to begin a thoughtful survey and analysis of works of modern landscape architecture and the designers who created them.

8 Charlene Roise, Hess Roise and Company, Lake of the Isles Master Plan: Document for Consultation (December 1999). This report includes a twenty-five-page assessment of significance for Lake of the Isles and Kenwood Park.

9 Introductory letter by Francis A. Gross, president, Board of Park Commissioners, in "Preface," *Minneapolis Park System*, 1883–1944.

10 Horace W. S. Cleveland, *Suggestions for a System of Parks and Parkways, for the City of Minneapolis* (Minneapolis: Johnson, Smith and Harrison, 1883), p. 4.

11 Garrett Eckbo, *Landscapes for Living* (New York: Duell, Sloan & Pearce, 1950).

12 "Historic Research and Analysis" from Allegheny Commons final draft, 27 August 2001, by Pressley Associates.

13 This report by Charles Davis, of 1 July 1867, was reprinted in the *First Annual Report*, pp. 28–29.

14 Eliza Smith Brown, "In Pursuit of a Breathing Place: A History of Allegheny Commons," prepared for the Garden Club of Allegheny County, September 1996, p. 26.

15 In 1927 Ralph Griswold moved to Pittsburgh, where he soon collaborated on Chatham Village with Wright and Stein. From 1934 to 1945 he was superintendent of parks, the first landscape architect to be employed by the City. Griswold is best known for his work on Pittsburgh's Point State Park, designed between 1946 and 1975. For additional information see the biographical essay by Behula Shah in *Pioneers of American Landscape Design* (New York: McGraw Hill, 2000), pp. 151–56.

16 Letter from John O. Simonds to Charles Birnbaum, 23 May 2001.

17 See the discussion of "Alterations and Additions" in *The Secretary of the Interior's Standards for the Treatment of Historic Properties with Guidelines for the Treatment of Cultural Landscapes* (Washington, D.C.: U.S. Department of the Interior, 1999), p. 53.

18 John O. Simonds, *Landscape Architecture: The Shaping of Man's Natural Environment* (New York: F.W. Dodge, 1961), pp. 228–29.

Preserve Some, Yes, But Also Improve, Add To, and Let Some Go

Laurie Olin

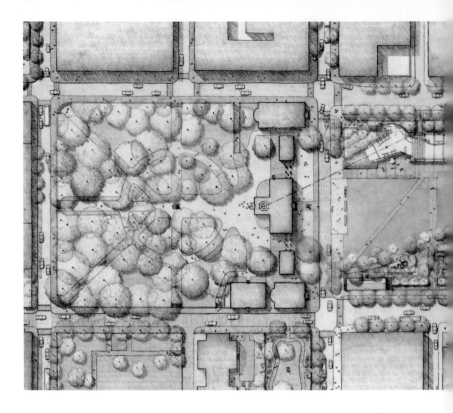

It is a cliché that landscapes are dynamic, not static. It is one of the differences between our medium and that of other arts, whether practical ones (functional, useful, instrumental ones like architecture) or fine arts such as painting or sculpture historically construed. Yet we have an urge to save and protect aspects of our environment that have become important, precious, and meaningful to us. This has led to conflict recently in the United States between those who value particular twentieth-century landscape designs and those who either do not value them or do not even recognize them. Recognition of and value for modern landscapes were the central topics of a conference at Wave Hill in 1995. One key question often skirted in that conference and in current debates regarding issues of preservation versus redevelopment is: *Must one always have to choose between the polar opposites of total change or no change?* Are there other choices? Isn't there a third way, one that isn't a compromise and pleasing to no one, not some sort of halfway mush, but a solution that is a both/and solution? While there are probably clear cases in which the only answer must be "no," I believe that there are many cases in which the answer is "yes" absolutely. Europe leads one to believe that the answer has oftentimes been "yes." Much remains of quality from the past, yet much that is absolutely new and of the highest quality is also produced and coexists beside, within, or around exemplary buildings, spaces, and landscapes from the past. How is this possible? What are the values, behaviors, and techniques responsible for producing this result?

Having practiced landscape architecture with my own firm for the past twenty-six years, I have been fortunate to design a considerable number

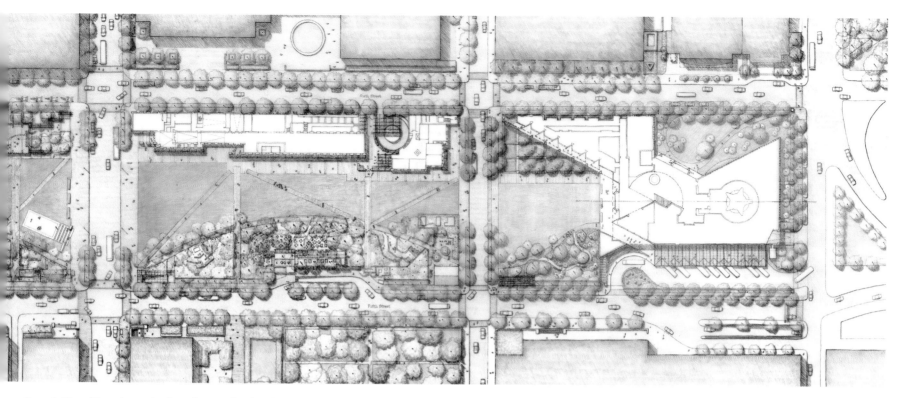

Figure 1. Plan of the redesigned Independence Mall with Independence Hall on the left (south) and the new Liberty Bell Center, Visitor Center, and Constitution Center respectively on the three adjacent blocks to the north; Kiley's design was on the northernmost block at the left. (Olin Partnership)

of projects which have been built. In that time, too, I have seen some of my own work destroyed, altered, replaced, or improved, and at the same time I have removed, altered, or added to the work of others. I have fought to help save particular works and have suggested, or gone along with, the alteration or demolition of the landscape and urban-design projects of others. I have probably made some mistakes along the way, but I believe I have also gotten it right on more than one occasion. The list of each of these categories is surprisingly longer than I'd thought. I am certain that this is true for a number of other practitioners my age. Making sense of such behavior and clarifying the issues seem useful, if only to help focus future efforts of those interested in the preservation of exemplary landscape design and those attempting to produce it.

Designers are agents of change. They are optimists, believing that they can make the world better in some way through their work. While this self-belief may be misplaced or unfounded in many cases, without it no one would go to the enormous trouble of being a landscape architect or architect. The principal activities of a landscape architect lie in determining what to keep, what to eliminate, and what to invent or add to a site—regardless of context, whether in rural, suburban, or urban situations, whether greenfield or brownfield. To do so, we must make judgments about the quality and purpose of a plethora of elements based upon values, based on the gamut of ecological and physical factors, historic, cultural, and artistic topics, economic, functional, and programmatic concerns. When change is proposed to any landscape, whether a modernist postwar design or somebody's farm, the first ques-

tion to ask is why this change? Do I agree with the premise that it can or should change? If so, how much and of what sort? What will be the net result? How does that compare with the current or former situation?

To make any sense of this topic, it is important that we consider why and how landscape changes are initiated and what the answers mean. The 1995 conference at Wave Hill suggested that the denigration and destruction of many modernist gardens begin with a lack of sympathy, often the result of ignorance. A low value is commonly attached to physical environments in general and to those of the recent past in particular (in whatever period). The actual decline, destruction, or disappearance of most landscapes does seem invariably to begin with physical neglect and lack of maintenance. In addition to abandonment, landscape designs can be destroyed by unsympathetic alterations, the degradation of context, and the development of a social situation that leads society to attack the setting in an effort to eradicate or displace the perceived problem. W. H. Auden's remark that a country gets the landscape it deserves is especially troubling because it acknowledges that we must want—and work to achieve—a high quality in the environment, just as in any other area of life. The implication, of course, is that not enough people in our society really give a damn about the things my profession makes.

Why, aside from neglect, are landscapes so dynamic and seemingly less stable than other aspects of our environment, such as buildings or historic works of art? The answer, of course, lies in the continual changes in society that create the economic, political, and social churning that at times has been called progress. Significant growth in population size forces the creation of new goods and dwellings, changes in transportation, architecture, institutions, and business. These in turn lead to pressure upon resources, whether they be tungsten and oil or open space for development of additional or new uses, and to competing demands upon capital available for investment, construction, and maintenance. Nearly all of the institutions, commercial operations, and residential areas that I have been associated with in my life have been in the process of changing in some of these many ways. Then, too, there are fashions in every human activity, from medicine and transportation, to clothing and garden design. Our society appears to long for stability, stimulus, and change in nearly equal portions. Americans are also restless and obsessed with newness.

Turning to specific examples that illustrate many of these issues, consider the following projects in which my office has confronted changes to three significant designs by Dan Kiley. These are the third block of Independence Mall in Philadelphia, the Nelson Atkins Museum grounds and sculpture park in Kansas City, and Lincoln Center in New York City. While it may seem strange that we have been asked to intervene in so many noteworthy sites, it actually makes sense. Historically prominent or established landscape architects, if they have the good fortune to practice for any length of time, will likely be called upon to work at sites where other notable landscape architects have worked. This is largely because these sites are likely to be the locations of powerful institutions, wealthy families, or important urban centers that are dynamic, growing, and able to indulge in changes of fashion. One has only to think of all the sites where Capability Brown followed and replaced or altered the works of Henry Wise and Charles Bridgeman, only to be followed and altered in turn by Humphry Repton, or even more recently by Russell Page. In our own era, how many of my colleagues, as well as my office, have found ourselves involved in some new transformation of one campus after another where the Olmsted Brothers worked? Where there is energy, power, money, and ambition, we find pressure for change, whether mere growth and addition or wholesale replacement of buildings and landscape.

Dan Kiley is one of my heroes. Rich Haag, who briefly worked for Dan in Vermont, introduced us to his work when we were students. I had the pleasure of being the first person to coax Kiley to come back to teach at Harvard in 1985, after decades of open disdain on his part. The studio that he offered concerned the redesign of the Mall in Washington, D.C., the current form of which is the result of the McMillan Commission's plan of 1910. Its principal authors were Frederick Law Olmsted, Jr., Daniel Burnham, and Charles Follin McKim. Their work, in turn, had replaced the residue of a never fully executed plan of A.J. Downing and Calvert Vaux. Kiley is an eminence, one of our greatest landscape architects, whom I respect and whose work I have studied scrupulously. I have also had the pleasure of collaborating with him on a marvelous project we did together with Richard Meier in Houston. It unfortunately didn't get built. Therefore, it is not lightly and without consideration that I presume to work on schemes that alter or replace his efforts.

Independence Mall, Philadelphia, Pennsylvania At this moment, the third block of Independence Mall, which once held 700 honey locust trees and a bevy of fountains in a geometric arrangement reminiscent of both the Tuileries in Paris and the Court of the Oranges in Seville, is a construction site for a large building. Its purpose is devoted to the interpretation of the United States Constitution. There is also an outdoor bus terminal with a small green park. This area is a portion of a larger redevelopment plan our office developed in response to a general management plan that was prepared by the National Park Service. It called for the complete redevelopment of a three-block-long mall stretching north of Independence Hall. My former partner, Robert Hanna, along with others, protested the demolition of this particular product of Kiley's. I will admit that when I first saw it in the autumn of 1968, I thought it was lonely and bleak. By the 1970s I had come to see it as lovely, but forlorn. By 1998 it was a ruin, the victim of a disastrous context, a decade of maintenance neglect, and subsequent mangling by the National Park Service. Deprived of people and use by a series of highway projects and the deadly government buildings that surrounded it, this block languished and was derided by City officials from Mayor Ed Rendell, who wanted to build hotels there, to National Park Service personnel who longingly wanted to use it for a maintenance facility. Due to abandonment in the late 1970s, the fountains had not worked for years. Pavements had come apart. Many of the trees were dying because of poor site preparation and construction procedures. Even the homeless population was sparse. After the National Park Service ripped out the paving, planted grass, and turned the fountains into planters, their own historians

Figure 2. *Kiley plan for the third block of Independence Mall (Office of Daniel Kiley)*

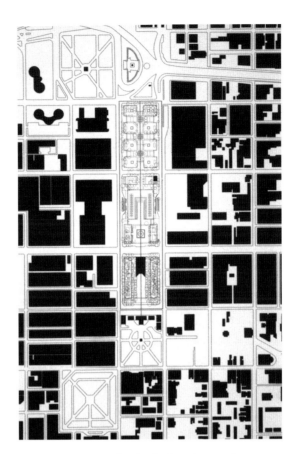

Figure 3. *Figure/ground study of Independence Mall in its urban context with 1976 Liberty Bell Pavilion on first block and Kiley plan on block three (Olin Partnership)*

Figure 4. *The third block of Independence Mall, 1975 (Office of Daniel Kiley)*

declared that this block had neither integrity nor historic value. At one time, years earlier, Dan had disowned it to me in conversation. He claimed that Harbison Hough Livingston and Larson, the architects who documented much of the project, and the City authorities had bastardized his design by deleting all the runnels he'd proposed. (These runnels would have made it more closely resemble the Court of the Oranges.) This site has undergone numerous changes in the past. I would be surprised if the version currently under construction lasts more than thirty years without further modification, largely because of the new interest and activity that our plan will bring to it but partly because of the reinvigoration of this historic part of Philadelphia.

Could Kiley's design have been reused in our plan? No, because the program to repair the gash in the city caused by the park in the first place (several hundred buildings were demolished to create it) called for putting back urban fabric—that is, erecting buildings with active facades and visitors, in this case, a 250,000-square-foot structure and a tour-bus facility. Could these new functions have been located elsewhere? Probably yes, but not without displacing some other program requirement and leaving this site to remain the problem it had become. I, too, came to the conclusion that Dan's park was ruined. If rebuilt, it would fail again because it was a serious urban-planning mistake, one that weakened the Penn Plan and the city.

Nelson Atkins Museum of Art and Henry Moore Sculpture Garden, Kansas City Done in collaboration with a dear friend of mine, the architect Jaquelin Robertson, this was and still is to large extent one of Kiley's major works. Several aspects of it are as beautiful as they are powerful and calm. I was happy to be a member of the ASLA design awards jury that gave it an Honor Award. Several years ago, however, the director and trustees of the museum, in an effort to solve the problem of growth in their collections, the increasing needs of curators and staff, and the burgeoning programs of a contemporary institution, concluded that they needed a major expansion. Robertson's firm was retained to develop the program and an invited competition between prominent young architects was held. Although the competition brief had located the site for the addition to the north of the existing Beaux Arts building, away from Kiley's terraces, lawn, and allees, Steven Holl proposed arraying most of the new structure(s) to the south, in effect replacing one of the sheltering arms of groves and berms that Kiley had created. A beguiling and striking composition, part in the earth and part rising out of it, Holl's scheme was selected by the museum leaders. As the architects were nearing completion of schematic design, our office was asked to come help resolve issues arising from this work, largely to do with the destabilization of the composition of the sculpture garden and issues of landscape over structure. Kiley, who had aged considerably in

19

Figure 5. Aerial view of Nelson Atkins Museum with Kiley and Robertson's
Henry Moore Sculpture Garden (Aaron Kiley)

Figure 6. Nelson Atkins sculpture garden in 2000 (Laurie Olin)

the past several years, was too infirm to be able to deal with it himself. Robertson, outraged by the museum's choice and Holl's proposal, urged me to take the commission to help try to pull things back together.

Engaging Rick Scholl, the same local landscape architect who had worked with Dan and the museum on the previous project, we embarked upon a collaboration, albeit after the fact, with Steven Holl, his staff, and the museum. Our efforts have been, largely, to knit the circulation back together, to save several of the destabilized Moore environments, and then to take some of the character of the Kiley wrapper to the north in a compensating move. It was a project in which the tasks were primarily to adjust, save, extend, screen, infill, excise, and generally work in a series of incremental moves. At the same time, we put one of Dan's original ideas back on the table with the museum and Holl: to continue the landscape, albeit in a somewhat revised form, across the road to the south to connect with a major creek and recreation trail. While we worked fairly well with the architects, finances for the project have proved to be difficult. At the moment, although construction is under way, we are not involved in the project. We have hopes of being asked back to help with the actual resolution of several key interfaces between the new architectural work and the earlier landscape. I believe that, if done well, this project can achieve the rich, layered qualities encountered so often in Europe, where one finds superb work from different periods in close proximity, often virtually one atop another. In that case Kansas City will be fortunate to have large amounts of Steven Holl and Dan Kiley (with a dash of us) rather than only one or the other.

Lincoln Center for the Performing Arts, New York City

The general story of the design and transmogrification of Kiley's work at Lincoln Center was told rather forcibly by Ken Smith at the 1995 Wave

Hill conference. Like Ken, I was disturbed a few years ago when Lew Davis of Davis Brody asked me to consult on the problems posed by the clumsy and ugly Milstein Bridge that connects the Julliard School to the Vivian Beaumont Plaza. I discovered that my favorite space at Lincoln Center, with its serene reflecting pool, one of the best Henry Moore sculptures in a public space (anywhere), and delicious weeping willows and bosquettes of London plane trees, was languishing. The planes had been replaced by dopey pear trees. The stone pavement was cracking. The willows had disappeared. I suggested that the bridge be converted into a green terrace with a café for the students and public overlooking this plaza and that the willows be restored—the sort of idea that I was able to accomplish later on a couple of projects in London. My suggestions were dismissed. So was I.

In January 2001 my firm was invited to join the architectural firms of Cooper, Robertson and Beyer Blinder Belle on a major planning study for the renovation, rehabilitation, and improvement of Lincoln Center. A month later, Frank Gehry and his staff joined us. It was a complex and difficult project both technically and politically. There were eleven different constituent clients, each of whom had a set of problems, needs, and desires and each of whom had a veto power over the entire project. Like the Articles of Confederation that preceded our Constitution, it was unworkable in terms of governance. The entire project was under a cloud. With our final presentation scheduled for September 11, it turned out to be doomed for the time being.

The project, however, attempted to come to terms with the fact that every building was seen as somewhat outworn and dysfunctional or in need of additional space from the perspective of the performing companies and their boards. This was borne out by voluminous architectural studies, some by members of our team, others by the firms of Skidmore,

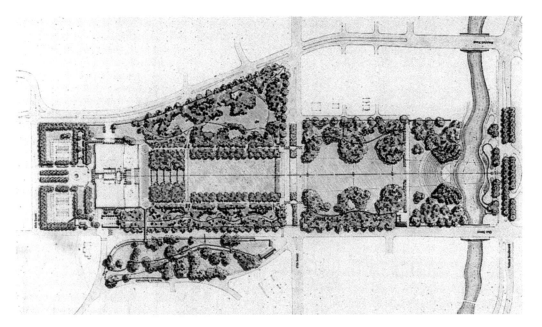

Figure 7 Plan of Kiley's proposal to extend the Nelson Atkins sculpture garden south to meet a regional trail and creek (Office of Daniel Kiley)

Owings & Merrill, James Stewart Polschek, and Bill Rawn. The well-known white travertine-clad buildings, now approaching forty years old, were created in a period that wasn't necessarily our best for the design and construction of buildings or mechanical systems. So, too, the public open spaces have their problems. As is often the case, the landscape at Lincoln Center was just about all that the disputatious inhabitants had in common. It became apparent that these spaces could be the glue to hold the disparate parts together. It also became clear that these spaces were no longer particularly nice or socially effective. While the separate organizations might or might not be able to achieve all their individual goals, it was incumbent upon Lincoln Center Incorporated and the design team that the public open spaces be revised and improved—probably radically so.

Admittedly, at night when the lights are on in the Halls there is a certain amount of glamour to Josie Robertson Plaza, as the central fountain court is officially named. Then the three theaters framing the space become transparent and people are silhouetted on all of the various levels as they move about the plaza. In the daytime, however, it is neither lively nor beautiful. It is as dead as the office-building plazas of the same era that it so closely resembles. Upon close scrutiny of both program needs (summer festival, benefit events, winter schedules, Big Apple Circus, etcetera) and the state of the current spaces, I concluded that a major overhaul was in order. Damrosch Park was more than a mess. It was a failure. Although designed by the distinguished firm of Innocenti and Webel in a manner intended to make it harmonize with the plaza designed by Kiley (on the other side of the Metropolitan Opera), it was neither a park nor a decent place to perform. In recent years, it has been filled with tents, trailers, clowns, and horse manure for months at a time. The circus had become, de facto, one of the resident performing tenants. Sound had to be electronically broadcast for summer music programs, partly because the band

shell reflected sound about twenty-five feet up on the side of the New York State Theater. As in Kiley's North Court most of the trees were in clunky raised stone boxes. It was a poor performance venue.

The central fountain court was also a poor effort. Clearly both fountain and pavement could be much better. How about seating? There is none. Then there is the riddle of the front entry of the center and the steps and ramps, which are really on Amsterdam Avenue, not Broadway, a hundred feet away. There is also the hideous Milstein Bridge and Julliard's own remote walkway and deck with its peculiarly tortured connections to street and subway. Despite the importance of Lincoln Center to the performing arts and the romanticism and nostalgia associated with the architects who designed it, there is hardly a less felicitous set of public spaces in New York.

Finally, and what concerns us here, there is the North Court designed by Dan Kiley. The more I tried to put forward a restoration or modest revision to the earlier scheme of Dan's with an emphasis upon transformation of the bridge to Julliard overlooking it, the more resistance I got. Why do they hate it so? I wondered. With the exception of Gordon Davis, the president of Lincoln Center, who was to depart in the middle of the project, and myself, it really is not loved by many at Lincoln Center. As I dug into what those who work there felt and thought, I learned how insecure each of the venues was. The management of Lincoln Center Theater, housed in the Vivian Beaumont, was convinced that no one could see them—a variation on the old "trees hide my sign" whine of merchants since Pompeii. They felt that the pool took up the space that they wanted to use for other uses, namely expansion of their lobby and events. The Julliard School holds receptions and parties on the horrid bridge because they have no land. They felt they could use the Kiley court. The Library folks, along with those in the Beaumont, felt that Kiley's tree boxes, a

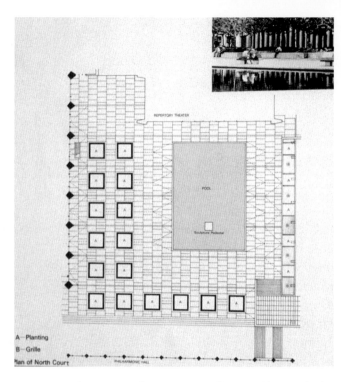

Figure 8. Lincoln Center North Court with additional willows (Office of Daniel Kiley)

Figure 9. Lincoln Center North Court as originally designed by Daniel Kiley (Office of Daniel Kiley)

motif in his work for better or worse, even with the planting of single pear trees, impede access and block views to their entries, and so on. Collectively they were determined to change this space to suit their perceived individual needs.

Along the way, we produced several versions for Damrosch Park. My favorite was like nothing in New York, or anywhere else really, but it didn't (purposefully) accommodate a circus, which in my view could be located on any parking lot in town. The version we finally settled on could be a very good neighborhood park, would be adaptable to performances, and will accommodate a circus. For the front plaza, we proposed ripping out the upper drive, pulling stairs and pavement out to the streets, and in the center creating a truly remarkable fountain or sculptural object around which people could actually sit. And yes, we did propose covering it (which would have been fabulous), but not with a silly dome, as *The New York Times* kept reporting.

Finally, to rescue the North Court, Frank Gehry and I proposed elimination of the Milstein Bridge, opening the court out to the street with a big stair that had trees descending with it, and a transformation of Sixty-fifth into a street with doors, windows, marquees, and signs—a street of theaters and performing-arts houses. We put back a smaller pedestrian bridge, proposed to be largely of glass. I also proposed a café with tables and chairs. Julliard quite rightly kept worrying about its campus. Where would its students hang out? Where would the school have its ceremonial events? While I kept fighting for the pool with its Henry Moore, the tenants, users, and managers kept arguing for fewer trees and less pavement, even lawn, which I felt was completely inappropriate. As everyone

who followed the psychodrama in the newspapers knows, it's a long way from over. I still believe that there is a way to regain much of the spirit of Kiley's space while accommodating the adjacent institutions, even making it a better place than Saarinen, Harrison, Beluschi, Johnson, and Kiley produced. There is a third way. I am hoping to have another crack at it again later this year.

What do my experiences at Independence Park, Kansas City, and Lincoln Center make me think? Many issues raised by Ken Smith, Charles Birnbaum, and others at the 1995 Wave Hill conference are still very troubling. Problems regarding the removal or transformation of twentieth-century landscape designs remain. While in some cases this is lamentable and preventing it from happening would be desirable, in others there are good reasons why change takes place. At Independence Mall, the entire park was misconceived. It has failed socially and artistically. Strangely beautiful as Kiley's third block was for a brief period, one would have had to rebuild an entire portion of the city around it in very particular ways (removing several government buildings and a highway and replacing them with mixed-use residential and commercial structures) in order to make any sense out of it. This was never in the cards. Although formally impressive, it was not connected to the society or historic situation in which it was placed.

Kansas City is a different story. Here was a gorgeous work that was loved and made sense. We have attempted to save and strengthen it, as much as possible, after the owner had already begun to alter it. We have even attempted to retrieve and promote a significant portion of Kiley's unexecuted initial proposal.

What will happen at Lincoln Center is still unclear. While I believe that there are ways whereby important aspects of the North Court's former qualities of delight, tranquility, and even spatial order can be recalled or represented in a new and different composition that solves the needs of the many constituents that wish to use it, I have no delusion that the original can or will ever be restored to its 1965 state. It is gone now. The intention of Lincoln Center Incorporated, the responsible umbrella organization, is to rebuild in a manner that caters to the demands of the residents and performing-arts tenants of this era. This was no fault of Kiley, who produced the only truly beautiful and lovable outdoor space at Lincoln Center.

Time and society can be randomly cruel and bountiful. Some of the best works of the past have disappeared, and some have remained, by accident, as well as on purpose. Many portions of the environment that come down to us through time were saved because they ended up in a backwater, out of the way of social change and the pressures of economic health and power. One thinks of the entire French Quarter in New Orleans or of Society Hill in Philadelphia, both of which survive nearly intact because they became slums while new development went elsewhere and were only rediscovered at a time when they could be appreciated. The works of the recent past are always in more jeopardy than those that are more venerable, partly because they are the results of one's parents' generation, partly because they are almost always located at or near the current locus of business and institutional activity. The competition for space and use is enormous in our cities. The destruction, rebuilding, and recycling that we find natural in forests is shocking when it happens in cities to landscapes and buildings that we recognize as having been created in our own lifetimes. Living in America at this moment, we cannot comprehend the enormous energy that is churning through what has become the largest economy and most powerful country in world history. How to direct and control change is the biggest challenge facing us on many fronts.

By coincidence it was exactly thirty years ago this autumn that I went off to Europe on two fellowships to study what I entitled "Continuity in the Landscape" in Britain and Italy. In my grant applications, I offered the proposition that Seattle (my home at the time) had attained a state similar to that of Rome in the sixteenth century, Paris in the seventeenth century, and London in the eighteenth century. A whole and complex city had come to exist with a full complement of infrastructure, industrial, residential, commercial, cultural, and artistic elements. Any new development would have to be overlaid upon this existing fabric, and in so doing, editing was called for. Some things, including infrastructure and open space, would have to be eliminated, some altered, some absorbed into larger structures, and some transformed. Often such changes called for increased scale and complexity. I wanted to see, study, and reflect how this had been done, for I knew it had been done both badly and well. I came away knowing that there were no rules, that this, too, was an artistic problem. Certainly layering was part of the answer. Inclusion and contrast were also part of the answer. Also, I realized that not all things were of equal value and that value judgments had to be made. Saving everything is as foolish and destructive as tearing everything down. Not all work by interesting or important figures is equally good and well made. The list of truths and issues is long.

Ars longa vita brevis. Reflecting on the work of our office these past twenty-five years, I can honestly say that these very issues have rarely been far from my mind. How else could I dare to work in cities such as New York or confront the dilemmas posed by clients who own and don't understand the works they possess, especially when they have been created by my teachers and mentors? So we must be brave enough to fight to save things, to change things, and to let things go.

Laurie Olin, FASLA, is the founding partner of Olin Partnership, Philadelphia, Pennsylvania. His many design projects include Bryant Park and Wagner Park in New York, the Getty Center in Los Angeles, and currently the redesign of the grounds of the Washington Monument in Washington, D.C.

BIBLIOGRAPHY

A few readily available sources that survey the work and career of Daniel Urban Kiley are:

Dan Kiley and Jane Amidon. *Dan Kiley, The Complete Works of America's Master Landscape Architect.* New York: Little Brown and Company, 1999; pages 42–43: for the third block of Independence Mall, pp. 56–57 for Lincoln Center for the Performing Arts, and pp. 112–17 for the Nelson Atkins Museum of Art and the Henry Moore Sculpture Garden.

Dan Kiley and Frederick Gutheim. *Landscape Design: Works of Dan Kiley. Process Architecture*, 33, 1982: pp. 106–107 for the third block of Independence Mall and pp. 56–59 for Lincoln Center for the Performing Arts.

William Saunders, ed. *Daniel Urban Kiley: The Early Gardens.* New York: Princeton Architectural Press, 1999.

Marc Treib, ed. *Modern Landscape Architecture: A Critical Review,* Cambridge: The MIT Press, 1993.

Peter Walker and Melanie Simo. "The Lone Classicist," *Invisible Gardens: The Search for Modernism in the American Landscape.* Cambridge: The MIT Press, 1994.

Warren T. Byrd and Reuben M. Rainey. *The Work of Dan Kiley: A Dialogue on Design Theory.* Charlottesville: The University of Virginia School of Architecture, 1983.

Modern Landscape at Risk

Stuart O. Dawson

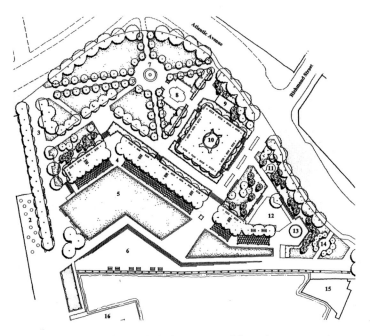

Figure 1. Boston Waterfront Park, built in 1976 to celebrate the Bicentennial, was awarded the ASLA Medallion Award during the 100th anniversary of the ASLA, celebrated in Boston. (Courtesy, author)

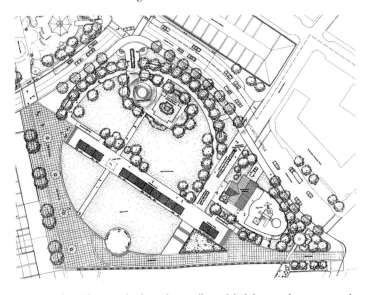

Figure 2. The Halvorson plan has substantially modified the award-winning Sasaki Associates plan for Boston Waterfront Park. (Courtesy, author)

When I became a landscape architect in the late 1950s there was an underlying belief, among most of us, that landscapes, once built, were forever. I toured Central Park. I visited classic and modern works at home and aboard. I was most influenced by Jensen's work in the Midwest; by Eckbo and Church; and by newcomers Kiley, Sasaki, and Halprin. As a dedicated landscape architect I was terribly optimistic. I realized that architecture, paving, and grading have an immediate impact and that landscapes take more time, but I also believed that new landscapes would be taken care of and be given an opportunity to mature, as envisioned by the designer. Let me share some reflections on these beliefs.

John Deere, a corporate headquarters in Moline, Illinois, supports my optimism. We have worked with this company for more than forty years. An institution, The First Church of Christ, Scientist, in Boston has confirmed my optimism as well. While we have not had the continuous continuity enjoyed at Deere, others including Larry Zuelke, Gary Hilderbrand, Douglas Reed, and Ann Beha have provided thoughtful stewardship.

But I have suffered a severe erosion of optimism with the loss of great works such as Jacob Riis by Paul Friedberg and of others, including our own Boston Waterfront Park. Is it that public works are harder to preserve and protect? Perhaps!

Waterfront Park is being demolished as we speak. In spite of numerous awards and an ASLA Medallion designation as well as a silent majority of support, the public client (with landscape architects on staff) and the "designer" (lots more landscape architects) have been dedicated to the total demolition of the original design. The word "restoration" is not in their vocabularies!

There is some irony in the demolition and redesign of the first Boston Waterfront Park. It was designed for the community and to celebrate our nation's Bicentennial. It was dedicated with GREAT fanfare in 1976. People and tall ships were everywhere! For the recent celebration of the ASLA's Centennial in Boston, Boston Waterfront Park was recognized as one of 362 significant works by landscape architects across the entire United States. That's 362 works over a 100-year period. Now there will be only 361. Should Medallion designation be a first step in establishing priorities for National Historic Landmark designation? Why not?

Consider works by Sasaki Associates in New York City. What is their future? I.P. Plaza, between Forty-fifth and Forty-sixth streets, is larger than a typical vest-pocket park. Will it be adopted? No, it is being demolished as we speak! Is it of sufficient "quality" to become a landmark? Perhaps, but it is too late! Hideo Sasaki was the lead designer. And there's Greenacre Park on Fifty-first Street, inspired by Paley Park and almost the same size. Could it qualify for landmark status? Again,

Figure 3. *This segment of the Sasaki design, the lamella truss, which parallels the harbor esplanade, has been removed by Halvorson, exposing a plastic playground and intrusive maintenance building. (Cymie Payne)*

Figure 4. *For more than thirty years local consultants have respected I. M. Pei's and Sasaki Associates' original plans for the Christian Science Center in Boston. (David Akiba)*

Figure 5. *For more than forty years John Deere and Company, along with the original architect and landscape architect, has built upon the original concept. (Alan Ward)*

Figure 6. *At John Deere, the Henry Moore hill sculpture, added twenty years after the original construction, was sited by Stuart Dawson of Sasaki Associates. (Courtesy, author)*

Hideo Sasaki, assisted by Masao Kinoshita, was the lead designer. Alice in Wonderland in Central Park, well over forty years old, will probably be there forever. Fernando Texidor was the sculptor and Hideo Sasaki, the landscape architect.

Perhaps, with Charles Birnbaum's leadership, we can stop the willful and deliberate demolition of works like Jacob Riis and Boston Waterfront Park. In a letter to me following some agonizing exchanges, Paul Friedberg wrote:

> Dear Stu,
> Thanks for your note. Yes, I'm irritated too—or better yet out-raged. The decisions to destroy these seminal works are made by officials that have no knowledge or understanding of what they

are doing. This isn't a battle that we—you and I—can take on alone. I think that the ASLA should voice their outrage and require that there be some method of evaluation in the decision-making process. The existing work that is not protected by the Landmark Law should be subject to some sort of third-party evaluation before it is destroyed. A committee of local professional societies and government agencies is one possibility. I would be happy to work on this with you if you're interested. But first we need the power of numbers that the ASLA provides.

Stuart Dawson, FASLA, is a landscape architect, urban designer, and a founding principal of Sasaki Associates, Inc., Watertown, Massachusetts. His international career encompasses major award-winning urban and waterfront developments, college and university campuses, museums, resorts, and corporate headquarters.

Then and Now

M. Paul Friedberg

M. Paul Friedberg

Figure 1. Water play at Riis Plaza Park, New York, New York, 1965 (All photographs, Office of M. Paul Friedberg)

To quote Genghis Khan: "Having a passion for your work is to be privileged and blessed. It is where the magic is." While accepting the philosophy but not the methods, I too have been privileged and blessed. I've experienced the magic working in this creative profession this past forty-eight years, further blessed by practicing during one of its most seminal periods. Based on the ability to survive and flourish during this exciting period, I've been asked to set the stage for today by providing a historical context for "the good old days."

Professionally I've been an advocate for change. Having said that, I admit that I'm sorry to see aspects of "the good old days" pass. That is the focus of my comments. You have been viewing change without the benefit of historical foundations—which means that you tend to rely on style and not substance. Although most of the papers in this collection of essays are made by advocates for the preservation of particular developments, this paper focuses on the preservation of ideas. Hence, I would like to propose the preservation of recently acquired values and philosophies that set the profession on a new course during the latter part of the twentieth century—values that provide the profession a dynamic new direction. I would like to revisit the gift from a few pioneers who took the profession kicking and screaming into the American city—a reflection of "the good old days." I will also conclude this nostalgic portion with a critical view of the current state of the profession. All this without a net. The powers that govern would not allow me to show my work. The work of others, yes, if necessary, but not my own. This is like asking me to fly without a plane. So, allow me, although restricted to words and whatever bias that comes with age, to take you on a personal journey about a time and space from the 1950s to 2000.

This was an especially dynamic period as landscape architecture, due to the efforts of a few pioneers, grew from an elitist group of estate designers and a fledgling ragtag group of individual practitioners into a significant, recognized, and respected profession. However, to take this beyond mere nostalgia or entertainment it is critical that we establish a common point of reference or baseline. We need a common definition of the profession. Without this commonality of view we cannot enjoy perspective, and any assessment of the future role of this profession is merely personal.

Purpose is and has been my baseline, my motivation, and source of inspiration. It is the rationale that precedes involvement. Think about it for a moment. Why would anyone choose this underpaid and misunderstood profession when there are many other compelling possibilities with greater recognition and economic rewards? Some are seduced by the term "landscape" and envision themselves embracing plants and assigned to the great outdoors, sadly to discover that they are shackled to a drafting board or computer. However, some get it from the beginning and have a clear sense of purpose—service to the public—a concept introduced by our revered founding father, Olmsted.

I pronounce his name with a hushed and reverent voice. Imagine me quoting Olmsted. Our leader suggested through his work and writings that purpose and self-justification are achieved through recasting open space for the benefit of the public. He proposed that the purpose of landscape architecture is to design environments that support community and encourage culture to flourish. Community is a socially based construct, and culture defines the human creative achievement. Even though it would be a stretch to see me as Olmstedian, I accept this purpose upon which the philosophical foundation of the contemporary profession is founded and structured. However, there is a kicker: How do we serve the public? "The public" is comprised of people, warts and all, and as we know from experience people are unreliable because they are subject to change. Olmsted sought to bring nature to the people to purge their souls of the contamination of the city. But times were "a-changing" and divesting themselves of this Victorian construct.

Currently the ART of the landscape architect—that which defines us—is our ability to manipulate and process open space to illuminate nature in the environment as well as our own unique nature. This is achieved through a mystical process of generating ideas called design—mystical because no one has convincingly determined the source of an idea. Open space is our medium, and aesthetic expression or beauty is the ultimate goal. In the end beauty has to be the critical and defining achievement. For without beauty we have no art and possibly no profession. Our purpose might better be

Figure 2. Trees and grass panels prior to the Friedberg design at Riis Park

served by engineers, environmentalists, or behaviorists, because ours is an applied art, separating and distinguishing us from the fine artist. We are constrained from allowing beauty to prevail over purpose. Self-serving decisions that interfere or inhibit the function of social and cultural institutions violate our purpose. We are not provided the liberty or freedom of the fine artist. The artist seeks purpose through a personal commentary on society, material, or whatever. We may share the same palette, collaborate and complement each other, but our purposes are not coincident. Ours is proscribed by and held hostage to the public need and will.

Purpose may be the constant, but the product, the results of our work, tends to be a moving target, for product results from necessity and necessity from context. So, as much as we revere and admire the philosophy of our predecessors, we cannot rely on their product to be universal and remain forever relevant. For instance, Olmsted, Jens, and others were anti-urban. They sought to alleviate the impact of the harsh urban environment of the industrial period. The product was the romantic, naturalistic retreat providing access to nature for the great unwashed.

• The sixty-hour, six-day workweek created the need.
• In the Great Depression Stein, Wright, and others sought an alternative to the city through satellite greenbelt towns.
• Robert Moses in response to the automobile created the parkways for the recreational Sunday ride and playgrounds as custodial cages for children freed from the factories and mills by child-labor laws.

Today it is hard to see the parkway as recreational or the Moses custodial playground as a creative environment for children or the greenbelt town, which has morphed into the ubiquitous suburb, as relevant. Hopefully we have a point of departure and can commence the journey back to the middle of the 1950s. Following World War II an irrepressible pressure for change was building in our cities. When it was released it would structurally alter institutions and the city as we knew it.

We found the profession burdened with the obsolete Olmstedian baggage of the Arcadian retreat. I entered, or more correctly backed into, landscape architecture in the middle of 1954—to find a humble, invisible, unlicensed profession. It could hardly be called a profession. It possessed so little currency that even Harvard graduates were unable to receive Parks Department contracts without an architect or engineer as partner. Anyone with the will or arrogance could call himself or herself a landscape architect. So I did.

Fresh out of Cornell, lightly armed with a B.S. in Horticulture and a desire to work in New York City, I mistakenly thought landscape architecture was a good way to make a living.

California was where it was happening.

Church, Eckbo, and Halprin were leading the way and the Japanese garden was the rage. Anyone with a sack of white gravel, a twisted pine, and someone's back yard could christen himself a landscape architect. The only civic urban open space in the country was Rockefeller Center, a space dedicated to a skating rink. The American Society of Landscape Architects and the schools remained committed to Arcadian, Olmstedian compositions as "one design fits all," thus persisting in the profession's anti-urban bias. Cities were alien turf, unfamiliar and threatening. People inhabited cities and people were unpredictable. Plants were not. So the big money was on the plant.

The Depression and Depression mentality were over. The workweek was shrinking. Wealth, time, and mobility allowed for freedom of choice. The automobile depleted the city of middle-class families by giving birth to the suburbs. Eisenhower's highway network freed the production centers from the umbilical cord of railheads and the city. Television shifted information from the ear to the eye. Air travel diminished distance.

These are a few of the most obvious dislocations fostered by the impact of the new technologies. However, change simultaneously disrupts and enriches our lives. One of the most visible effects was reflected in the population of the city. It wasn't what it used to be. The lost manufacturing industry was replaced with service industries employing bright young professionals. The empty nester, freed of the social and economic burden of child raising, longed for excitement. The burbs were too passive. The city with its street life, entertainment, and cultural opportunities became the environment of choice.

New freedoms bestowed the opportunity to live and work as and where we wanted. As Tom Wolfe put it, "If I only have one life to live I'll live it as a blond"—or in the city. As a result landscape architects, stubbornly refusing to relinquish their death grip on Arcadia, were challenged to attend to this unfamiliar environment, the city, where they had to substitute people for plants. No longer were passive, romantic, rustic parks sufficient for this new population. Although loved and admired as a special place, the park was only one option—not capable of accommodating all the new demands. The new population sought the vitality of city life and had no intention of retreating from it. They were here by choice.

These urbanites were self-selected and coveted social interaction, intensity of street life, the sharing and participation. Why would they seek the Arcadian retreat as their sole recreational option? The city, a liability to some, was an opportunity for others. Entering this new frontier we find a new breed of landscape architect, one who marries people, places, and plants.

Figure 3. Pyramidal water features filter water at A.C. Nielsen Company, Chicago, Illinois, 1972.

Figure 4. Willow and pools at A.C. Nielsen attract wildlife.

Figure 5. Water changes elevations and creates spatial rooms.

Figure 6. Plaza spaces float over water pools.

Figure 7. 29th St. Playground, New York, New York

Figure 8. Waterfall at Park Place, Vancouver, British Columbia, 1982

Figure 9. Jeanette Park, New York, New York

Figure 10. Relaxing at Madison Mall, Madison, Wisconsin

The 1950s and 1960s set the stage for one of the most exciting and fertile periods this profession was to experience since its inception. Interestingly or sadly enough, this reorientation of the profession resulted from external pressures—the urban client, the new consumer of urban space—and not from professional foresight. With this new urban demography the profession was challenged to reconstitute itself and join a new approach to city planning and design. Invent, excite, create, or become obsolete: This was a call for those creative and adventurous among us and a rejection of the meek or conservative.

These were expansive times with few inhibitions. Challenged with this imperative emergence, the noble among us, Eckbo, Halprin, Sasaki, Kiley, Zion, and others—pioneers venturing into the city, armed only with intuition and passion and lacking any discernable precedent or tradition—took on the challenge. Guiding their dedication and purpose was the philosophical foundation of landscape architecture, a socially based applied art. They were the first to accept the city on its own terms, extrapolating Olmstedian principles to fit this new urban context. Out of their collective creative energies we were presented new ideas about the design of space, urban space. Exciting, innovative, and inventive urban forms emerge, truly American in origin: the Main Street mall, the vest-pocket park, the park plaza, the interactive fountain, and the greenway, forms that were fitted to the American temperament and urban fabric, innovative concepts and paradigms suggesting that urban space is neither proprietary nor independent, but integral to and an adjunct of the urban plan. Landscape architects became players in the design of city spaces. Some chose to expand the boundaries of the profession by collaborations with fine artists seeking a new approach to enrich the process and product.

Bob Zion was proactive. Without a client he proposed his invention, the vest-pocket park, stimulating the imagination of the public as patron. The results: Paley Park, arguably the most elegant urban space in the city.

I don't intentionally leave Ian McHarg out of this overview. Ian, a monumental figure in his own right, pioneered ecological planning. While essential to design, it doesn't directly relate to my focus. Ian had a love/hate relationship with designers. As a powerful force in his own right he almost single-handedly committed the profession to environmental planning, thereby bifurcating it. Well, that is a leapfrog synoptic glance at "the way it was."

Now, " the way it is" and "the way it can be." Rather than critically commenting, I would prefer to pose some critical questions and a few visions. The recent past provides the profession with a legacy of precedents relevant to contemporary practice—a legacy to build on. But what are the defining questions? Do we have a vision for the future? Any gain in numbers, recognition, and respect is of little value unless it can be employed to expand our creative abilities and influence.

What are our creative goals? What are the political, social, and cultural values that we support? How do we participate and provide positive direction for the process of change? For instance, State and City parks departments represent the largest developers of public space. What role do we have in monitoring or critiquing their activities? When was a design of the parks department recognized for its quality? Why aren't the most talented designers represented? Why are competitions for important public spaces ignored? The French have provided us with models of successful competitions, two unique parks, Citroen and La Villette. (I was invited to France to serve on the jury for La Villette.)

Little by little mindless, petty, myopic people make decisions that affect the profession and erode the quality of our public life—as well as destroy important sites. Do we or should we have a say regarding who guides us in the development and preservation of the public domain? We just installed a new parks commissioner. Without commenting on his qualifications or talents, what was our role in this selection?

The Hudson River and the East River waterfronts, New York's most important open-space resources—we're an island—are currently in planning and development. These riverfront parks will impact the future life of the city for generations. It is both interesting and sad that to date none of the architectural critics has commented publicly on the content or quality of these efforts. The waterfront offers vast opportunities for inventive and original thought and design-opportunities yet unfulfilled. Are we advocates of inventive and creative development possibilities like public/private partnerships? Is the integration of park and development an effective means of creating new and maintainable public amenities? Again Battery Park and Bryant Park are exceptional models.

Where are the critics of the city's open space? I enjoy the esoteric comments of the architectural critics, but for the most part these are intellectual exercises that do little to educate or build a constituency for a better public environment. Without discounting their value, they limit their focus to abstract issues and do not take on the realities of daily life. Without critics there can be little accountability. What other profession is allowed to affect the public without accountability or critical analysis? Are we not are the greenest of all the professions? And yet the architects have preempted "green design." We have good tools and a public sympathy for this new awareness, and with few exceptions there is silence.

Where are the landscape architects in the urban-design process? Are they informed and qualified? Is this a part of their education? If open space is not an integral system within the urban-design process we will continue to be relegated to design fragments of leftover space. And that is not where the magic is. Comprehensive planning and urban designs such as Battery Park are where the magic is. Our domain will continue to be trivialized unless we are players and are qualified to take part in the "big show." Open space, the public realm, is our territory. With it comes a unique responsibility that we have yet to fulfill as advocates of this realm. We need to dream and then fulfill our dreams. Our city should be realized as:

- a sculpture park freeing art from the museums, allowing us to live with—and not make pilgrimages to—our art;
- our arboretum, so that we can live with plants as our botanical counterparts, not as captives in planters. Let cherry, magnolia, and crabapple blossoms fill our streets;
- streets recast as pedestrian zones free of conflicts with automobiles.

It's out there waiting to be realized as a fulfillment of our dreams. The way has been paved and the legacy exists. We are obligated by our antecedents to hone our skills and seek to educate our partner—the public. They need to be made aware that they are being deprived. Without a public constituency all of the above are merely unfulfilled dreams.

I would like to conclude this call to arms with the mandate that we become the instruments in the shaping of our city and not let the city shape us. It is contestable whether age restricts or expands one's perspective, but what is uncontestable is the passion that Genghis refers to. That remains undiminished. The simple act of confronting another design challenge continues to nourish and enrich my life and through it hopefully the lives of others. Some of us created a past and a legacy that should be preserved as the foundation for the future.

Founder of the landscape architectural program at CCNY, author, and product designer M. Paul Friedberg, FASLA, is a dedicated urbanist and one of the first practicing landscape architects to confront the city on its own terms.

Social Force: The Urban Optimism of M. Paul Friedberg

Paul Bennett

Figure 1. Riis Plaza Park aerial view, New York, New York, 1965 (All photographs, Office of M. Paul Friedberg)

Two years ago I wrote an extended essay on Paul Friedberg that was published by the magazine *Land Forum*. In preparing that piece, I spent a lot of time with Paul, sharing coffee in his apartment on the Upper West Side of Manhattan and chatting for hours about everything from sculpture to psychology and, in fact, touching very little on landscape design. Friedberg is one of those loquacious souls who are literally bursting with energy, ideas, and exuberance to the point of overflow. He makes you a cup of coffee, sits you down brusquely, and, with his omnipresent pen and pad, unleashes a rapid-fire monologue that is as notable for its quantity as its range.

One of the first things you observe is that Friedberg loves tangents. He flies from one idea to the next, discarding such rules of the literary arts as transitions and logical setups and blowing a wide conceptual swath through the conversation. In one instance, he will toss out a rhetorical question fraught with implications. He says, "Tell me Paul, how do you think, in the absence of morality, we can motivate people to act responsibly?" While you are recovering from this, he has already focused on the minute detail of a new piece of playground equipment he is designing. This necessitates some mad scribbling on a cocktail napkin, for which in some circles he is mildly famous.

I do not want to give the impression that Friedberg is scatterbrained or unfocused in his thinking. Those who were here this morning heard him describe himself as passionate. This is undoubtedly a very apt assessment. However, after spending some serious time with Friedberg discussing landscape architecture and then spending some more serious time pouring through slides and visiting his landscapes, I have come to a different view. Friedberg possesses an unabashed optimism and an unwavering faith in humanity. This is an outlook that pervades every aspect of his work: the playlots he designed for housing projects in the 1960s, the public plazas he made in the 1990s, and, arguably, the corporate campuses and residential developments that have occupied him of late.

I will be consciously reining in my talk today to deal with Friedberg's early career when he established himself both as a major force in the profession of landscape architecture and also as an undeniable voice of modernism. I will paint a brief biographical portrait of him as a person, a thinker, and a designer and touch briefly on more recent work. Then I will return to his early work from the 1960s and look at what makes these modernist and why that is important. And finally, I will touch on the thorny issue of whether this designation necessitates a preservation ethic, and if so, of what kind.

Friedberg likes to say that he backed into the profession of landscape architecture. Although he was born in New York City during the height of the Depression, he grew up in rural surroundings, first in Winfield, Pennsylvania (where he remembers the teacher toting a shotgun with squirrels hanging from it) and then in Middletown, New York. After the Friedberg family moved to Middletown during Paul's early adolescence, his father started a nursery business that proved quite successful. Because his father was in poor health, Paul, for all intents and purposes, ran the family business. When he graduated from high school, it was not surprising that he attended the Agricultural College at Cornell University. The plan was for him to return to Middletown and become a nurseryman.

When Friedberg was first relating his life's story to me, I thought for sure that he would end up coming into contact with landscape architecture at Cornell, which then and now has an internationally recognized program. But it turns out that he, in fact, graduated with a degree in horticulture, having failed the only design class he ever took. For the most part, he was ignorant of landscape architecture. What did happen at Cornell was that Friedberg came into contact with the larger cultural landscape of art and learning, and over the four-year period he experienced a general broadening of his mind. As Friedberg describes it now, while at college, he fell in with an intellectual group that exposed him to art, history, philosophy, and literature. The result of this was earth shaking to a self-described bumpkin. One of the great things about the Ag program at Cornell, Friedberg told me, was that it enabled him to take classes outside the program, in the College of Liberal Arts. Today, in looking back at this formative period from the vantage (or disadvantage) of some five decades, Friedberg says that it was this brief contact with the wider world of ideas and intellectual history that eventually brought him to the front door of landscape architecture, instilling in him an intellectual curiosity and vigor that is, in his opinion, indispensable for a designer.

I think this is an important idea to linger over, especially in this context of modern design. The design arts are essentially a component of the liberal arts. Removing all the specialization of landscape architecture—the engineering, horticulture, drawing, etcetera—at base design is simply a study of the human condition. It provides a creative response to that condition in the same way that literature, painting, sculpture, and all the fine arts as well as history, philosophy, and all the humanities do. I would argue that such an open, experimental, philosophic view of design is especially a product of the modern period itself, born from an overwhelmingly positive faith in the ability of design to assess and correct the wrongs of the world.

It was not until he came to New York City looking for work as a horticulturist that Friedberg actually discovered landscape architecture. At the time the only job in landscape architectural offices for a plantsman

Figure 2. Children enjoy active play at Riis Park playground.

with his training was as a draftsman. Unfortunately (or fortunately, rather) Friedberg did not draw well. He soon ended up in the office of an architect named Joseph Gangemi picking out trees and shrubs for municipal projects. The work was horribly banal. However, one benefit Friedberg received was to make the acquaintance of a real-life landscape architect named Conrad Hammerman, who also worked in the office. Hammerman, a recent graduate from the landscape program at Cornell, became an influential force on young Friedberg. He exposed him to an expansive view of landscape architecture and its place within the context of intellectual and artistic history. When they were not wasting time between specification jobs in Gangemi's office, the two would talk about landscape. Friedberg now credits this as possibly the most formative moment in his career. Suddenly he came to realize that there was a tradition and philosophy to landscape architecture. There was something beyond trees and flowers called design. This was very exciting stuff. Friedberg's recollection of this backing into the profession has an air of insouciance, of improvisation, of self-invention—all hallmarks of the modern spirit: that the best designer is the one who comes to the discipline without preconceptions, blissfully ignorant, pure.

A trip to Europe ensued: a typical grand tour in which Friedberg visited all the major works of landscape, architecture, and other art forms that Hammerman had diligently listed for him. When he returned to New York, he quit his job and set up shop as a landscape architect from his apartment on the Upper West Side. He was twenty-eight years old and the year was 1959.

Friedberg spent his first few years in private practice doing commissions for the New York Housing Authority, frustrating work that required a landscape architect do little more than shuffle around a set of prespecified plants, paths, lights, and benches in a geometrical game, perhaps not all that different from such work today. He dabbled in this work for several years. In 1965 he heard about a competition sponsored by the

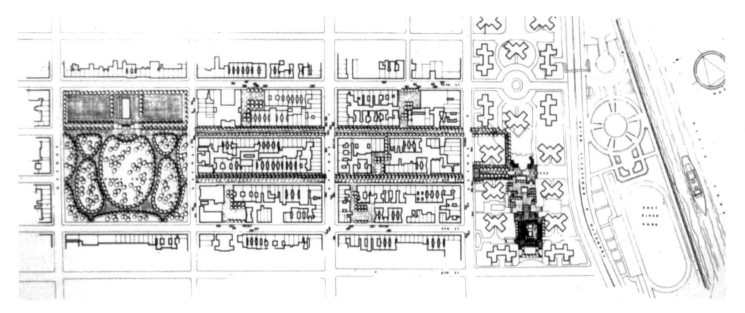

Figure 3. Site Plan, Riis Park

Astor Foundation to redesign the landscape of a Housing Authority complex on the Lower East Side. Friedberg entered the contest and teamed up with the architect Simon Breines. They won and were given a commission to design the Carver Houses. Breines, the more established practitioner, took the lead. Having produced a successful, pleasing design, the duo were given a second commission for another housing complex on the Lower East Side called the Jacob Riis Houses. It was on this latter work that Friedberg, at the ripe young age of thirty-four, was given the lead design role. In response to the challenge, he produced what would be viewed as perhaps the most forward-looking, innovative, and intensely urban landscape design of the day. The project quickly made him a star in the profession.

It is hard today, a mere thirty-five years later, to fully appreciate the impact Riis had on the professions of landscape architecture and urban design. In order to do so we have to transport ourselves back to that era and recall that despite the modernist revolutions that had taken place in the other arts over the previous fifty years, landscape architecture in the early 1960s was still stuck in the nineteenth century, especially where the city was concerned. In urban situations, design and planning ideas were still derived along Olmstedian lines. As Friedberg likes to say, the Arcadian model held sway. That may be a simplification of Olmsted's urban vision, but it is undeniable that in 1965 it was still generally accepted that the landscape architect's role in the city was to import images of the countryside, to make dioramas of nature, and to create a place of romantic respite where city-dwellers could take refuge from, as the poet Allen Ginsburg would inimitably phrase it around the same time, "the grooking city."

The design of Riis rejected this view. The landscape that existed when Friedberg arrived on the scene can best be described as Central Park-like: a park-bench-lined promenade shaded by trees ringing a large lawn that had turned to dirt from years of use. His redesign proposed something radically different, something architectural, hardscaped, and referring more to society than to nature. The spaces were tailored to people and human interactions. Friedberg would, on reflection, term this "the human ecosystem." There were obvious references to modern art and architecture in the Mondrian-like fountains and the orthogonal layout of the spaces. What was really forward-looking and new was how the landscape suggested that what people in a city really needed was not an escape to the country, but a better-functioning urban environment. Instead of denying the funkiness, the urbanity, of its surroundings, Riis tried to perfect them. It tried to serve the existing population and its needs rather than to meld that population and those needs with some ideal, Arcadian or otherwise. It was this that made Riis most characteristically modern. It was above all a functional landscape.

Friedberg's unflinching urbanism shocked a profession that was, as he notes, still focused on the suburbs. His influence among succeeding landscape architects who would come to the city was profound. Probably no one was influenced by this idea of landscape urbanism more than Friedberg himself. For the next thirty years, he would make a name for himself in the city as one of the foremost urban landscape architects.

I would like to focus for a moment on the playground as a form because, while Riis was hugely influential in terms of changing the way playgrounds would be designed through the remaining years of the1960s and 1970s, its lessons have since faded. Today's playground design is the product of the litigious decades of the 1980s and 1990s. It has retreated in the face of lawsuits into a womb of safety regulations. What we see today is basically a sandlot with a fancy prefab swing set in the middle looking a lot like playgrounds of the 1950s. In contrast, the Riis playground was stunningly imaginative. It reminds us of a time when playground design could be fertile ground for a designer of Friedberg's caliber.

Figure 4. Creative play on the granite igloo

Figure 5. Children enjoy the water spray fountains.

Figure 6. Park playground functions for multiple users.

Figure 7. Amphitheatre seating provides a resting spot.

As you can see from period pictures of Riis, one of the big ideas that Friedberg developed here was to discard the idea of play equipment as discrete objects in space, to conceive of the entire landscape as a source of what he would call "continuous play." As a result, the space becomes a connected experience of tunnels, slides, stone mounds, and metal climbing bars that challenge and beguile the children. Friedberg says that he was influenced by new theories of child development just becoming popular in academic circles at the time that offered new conceptions of how children learned from their environment. Such thinkers as R.D. Laing and Luther Gulick proposed that children learn from their entire environment. Even play can be a learning experience. Perhaps what goes on after school is more significant than what happens in school. What

strikes me, however, is not the visible presence of new development theories in the landscape. It is, rather, the raw exuberance of the design itself. This is a landscape that celebrates children, that celebrates people. There is a belief that landscape can make a difference. In the meticulously crafted earthforms, inspired by Noguchi and with an almost Arts and Crafts attention to detail, we can read a message to the effect that good design, if good enough, can actually ameliorate the ills of the city and lift people up.

Certainly this was the message picked up by the media that flocked to Riis for its unveiling. The New York papers arrived first. Then *Life* published a several-page spread on the park. It seems incredible today: a mainstream American magazine not only publishing an experimental landscape, but one that was part of a public-housing project. But this was an era when the fate of a city and its poor populations concerned the average person. It was an era when the nightly news paid attention when imaginative thinkers like Paul Friedberg came up with an innovative attempt to fix urban problems.

Unfortunately, despite the publicity and obvious fitness of design, Riis did not fare well. During the 1980s pandemics of drug abuse and crime, combined with a fiscally weak and politically neglectful Housing Authority, took their toll on the landscape. The play equipment eventually broke down. It was removed bit by bit. The water was turned off. The plant material died or grew out of bounds. Finally, in the late 1990s, the entire landscape was demolished and made anew by an in-house Housing Authority design team. The new design looks very much like the one that preceded Friedberg's modernist one: lawns, winding paths, and various other neo-Olmstedian landscape park elements that have become the vocabulary of the municipal design agencies in New York, comprising what is, to put it bluntly, possibly the most banal design work in the country. The new landscape also includes all the telltale signs of today's preoccupation with safety. It is, in Yi-Fu Tuan's phrase, "a landscape of fear." Everything is restrained, distrustful, and fenced in. People are controlled and told where to go and what to do or, rather, where not to go and what not to do.

Friedberg was never consulted or even informed about the redesign of Riis until well after the fact. When I asked him about this recently, I was surprised that he did not seem to harbor much resentment. Instead, he sort of huffed, shrugged his shoulders, and said something to the effect of "What can you do?"

Digging a little deeper, I began to read a different reaction. In the forty-plus years that Friedberg has been practicing landscape architecture, he has seen an amazing amount of change. Perhaps the biggest change, however, is what he characterizes as a moral retreat. The profession and its patrons today lack much of the courage or bravado, if you like, that they exhibited during the modernist decades. "Where is the experimentation?" Friedberg asks. Perhaps it exists in such corners of the discipline as ecology, political processes, and, in Friedberg's own new corner, the public-private development partnerships to make successful landscapes. But what about the human ecosystem, and what about the bold faith in humanity and optimism implicit in a place like Riis? Where are those landscapes today? I, unfortunately, did not get an answer from him.

One interesting question to ask about the demise of Riis: Why did it fall into neglect? (After yesterday's presentations, I wonder if the absence of a Henry Moore sculpture might be somehow to blame. Did

Figure 8. Children playing in fountain pools.

anyone notice that all the successfully preserved and maintained Modernist landscapes have a Henry Moore sculpture?) One potential answer, and this is one drawn from both Friedberg's own casual empirical research and my own impressions as a journalist covering landscape for the last five years, is that, outside of a handful of aesthetes and scholars, the average person feels very little love for modern design generally. In particular, I find that this antipathy runs deepest in terms of landscape. We hear all the time—and not just from critics looking to say something because that is what they get paid to do, but from average users—that modern landscapes are not friendly. They are cold, austere, and too abstract. We saw yesterday that even in the Miller garden, Mrs. Miller has resorted to planting flowers because, as the presenter related, she simply likes flowers in her garden. We might consider this as a kind of general axiom of anti-modernist sentiment: that people like flowers.

There were no flowers at Riis. In fact, one of the striking characteristics of the design was its eschewing of anything precious. Friedberg's aesthetic was robust modernism, not minimal per se, but a stark, visually striking, and architectonic composition. It was the city remade as landscape. But, again, people like flowers.

So when we talk about preserving modern landscapes, we need to realize that in addition to the winnowing of design by nature and time—by the natural and temporal processes that have the effect of purging landscapes of things that do not work botanically or culturally—there is also a kind of capricious attitudinal winnowing. By this I am referring to the public perception of landscapes and what might be called, at worst, the loathing of modern landscapes and, at best, malevolent neglect. Over time, despised elements are removed (experimental furnishings, sculptures, hardscape) and updates are brought in (shrubs to soften and romanticize the landscape, benches designed to prevent the homeless from sleeping on them, and, of course, flowers). To the landscape architect and landscape theorist, this looks like a bastardization, haphazard and wrong. But beyond the obvious aesthetic mistakes of the Housing Authority's revamping of Riis, it seems as though its designers were responding to a public complaint, one, I believe, we hear repeated throughout this country, a complaint against the inhumanity and coldness of modernism. Are we, as landscape architects and landscape theorists, blind to this complaint? Are we aware of this antipathy? Do we ask why it exists?

I want to end by addressing the central question of preserving modern landscapes. As has been noted previously, preserving modernism is, in itself, a funny idea, an anachronism. Modernism is nothing if not an unwavering view toward the future, if not an erasing of the past, at least a decisive, powerful departure from it. As a result, one of the gifts that modernism has bequeathed to us is the intellectual impulse to continue this movement forward, to erase and depart from the past. Friedberg is a quintessential modernist in this manner. I have tried in this paper to give a sense of his personality as well as his work. Never sentimental, he has always valued looking forward. His work, as much as the professional and philosophical attitude that has sustained him over four decades, epitomizes innovation and inventions, what I would call faith in the redemptive powers of design.

So one interesting question needs to be asked: Should works of modernism be preserved at all, since by preserving them we may risk killing their spirit? When I posed this question to Friedberg the other day, ever the maverick, he responded quickly and sharply: "You're right. We shouldn't preserve modernist landscapes."

I imagine that Friedberg's curt reply was in response to my question, which may have sounded to him like, "Hey, what do you think about us dipping you in amber here at this conference and hanging you on a hook at the MOMA?" Preserving modernism is dangerous because there are a lot of modernists walking around: Who in their right mind would want to be preserved? But, more deeply, I understood his answer to represent this idea of optimism that I discussed earlier as an attribute of his 1960s work. It pervades not only Friedberg's designs but also his entire world-

Figure 9. Children engage in continuous play on metal climbing apparatus and the granite igloo.

view. It is my belief that Friedberg's unpremeditated, Dadaist, improvisational approach to his career (and life in general) has informed his aesthetic, which I have described, alternately, as robust, optimistic, confident. Since he is always chafing against the staid and predictable, it should not be surprising that Friedberg resists the impulse to preserve his work. Other than a shrug and a sniff at the news that Riis is gone, what can he, as a quintessential modernist, do?

As a bystander and lover of great landscape, my own personal opinion is that Friedberg's seminal early work should be preserved. But I also worry that by museumfying a place like Riis, we may strip it of what made it unique to begin with, which was not the geometric fountains, the straight lines, the restrained planting palette, and other vestiges of modernist aesthetics. It was the spirit of the place: its bold, urbanist propositions; its now rare optimism. If it were somehow possible to preserve this ineffable spirit of a place, then I would say, sure, let us do it. Let us fight hard for places like Riis. But I think we need to first ask some serious questions. We need to think deeply about the fundamental propositions that modernism has made and the impact of that legacy. And maybe we should start by asking ourselves, Why do people like flowers so much?

Paul Bennett is a design journalist, former editor-at-large for Landscape Architecture *magazine, and a contributor to* Architectural Record.

Preserving the Designed Landscape

Lawrence Halprin

In the past few decades the need for preservation and conservation of our diminishing natural resources has become a major national issue. We recognize the need to save and protect our natural resources, and this important movement includes air, water, land, and biological species. Internationally, the urgency is even more apparent and has recently surfaced in the Kyoto protocol and at the United Nations meeting in Johannesburg. These movements are dedicated to the preservation of our planet and our biological way of life. They are fighting against thoughtless destruction and a mind-boggling pace of change.

In the natural environment we have also recognized the importance of specific natural networks: We are restoring watersheds, river systems, and forest habitats. We want to protect them as well as make them available for hiking, boating, fishing, swimming, etcetera.

And, still, we desperately need other types of preservation and conservation that affect our cultural as well as our environmental heritage. In the landscape of our cities, many important designed improvements, built since World War II, are beginning to come under attack by civic agencies and developers. Landmark-quality buildings as well as plazas and parks are being torn down to accommodate larger developments. Lands set aside for open space are particularly vulnerable and are often sacrificed for freeways or commercial malls. The argument for acquiescing to demolition is often based simply on the fact that "change is inevitable and we just have to put up with it."

The side effect of this point of view is that wonderfully designed open spaces are often sacrificed for what are perceived to be more "practical and needed" new facilities. What is particularly upsetting is that in the last few decades, the importance of cities and their public open space has undergone a roller coaster of attitudinal changes. At times, life in cities has been thought to be undesirable and frightening. During those times, open spaces become targets of our fear: Concrete is poured and high-powered lights are added to open spaces and parks. Presumably this is done to make them feel safer.

Eventually the pendulum swings and young people and empty nesters find their interest in living in cities renewed. They move back to cities partly to avoid long and increasingly arduous commutes. More importantly, they move back to enjoy the architecture, designed landscapes, streets, and open spaces as well as the rich cultural and social life that cities offer.

The quality and character of all cities is dependent on design. This includes the design of buildings and, perhaps more importantly, the design of open spaces (streets, plazas, parks, river edges, etcetera). These open spaces have been designed over time and all together are

Figure 1. Clear cutting of forests in the Northwest (Dai Williams)

what we term landscape architecture. The best pieces of landscape art and design are important not just as contemporary places to live in but as part of our history and culture. We travel to iconic places all over the globe and use them as touchstones for our culture and our memories. The difficult question is not whether we should protect and preserve the best of these designs, but which ones are the best. What is worth preserving and why? Not everything from the immediate past is worthy of preservation. How do we decide which works deserve to be preserved in our cultural landscape?

In the preservation of a major natural phenomenon and its elevation to the status of a national park or monument, the choice is a congressional one and based on specific criteria. But when a smaller open-space design is at stake, the selection has to be determined at a more local level. Here the issue is more complicated in a way, since the criteria are far more varied and subtle than those for the grand national parks. In cities, plazas and pocket parks are often judged as if they are pieces of

sculpture. Sometimes they are historical. As a result, decisions must be made with the assistance of a variety of specialists, art critics, elected officials, and commissions.

In the "fine" arts the processes by which decisions of cultural or artistic value evolve are very organic and almost imperceptible. Icons emerge slowly in literature, painting, music, and dance. In landscape architecture, however, critical issues often arise suddenly, and such decisions are often triggered by commercial agendas. It is, therefore, important to formalize a process for preservation that can react as quickly as the attack.

From my own experience here are some of the more important values for making preservation decisions.

Status in a community is one important consideration in all decision-making. Central Park in New York and Golden Gate Park in San Francisco are clear examples of landscapes that are essential to the identity and life of these cities. In the case of Central Park, the design itself is exemplary. That, plus the fact that it was designed by one of our

Figure 2. Sensory walk along the Gualala River during a "Creativity Workshop" (Brian Collett)

great landscape architects, makes it deserving of preservation. These two characteristics (status and exemplary design) should make a landscape at least worthy of consideration for preservation.

At its best, landscape architecture is an art form, whether a major designer or an unknown one produces it. Therefore, a panel of art critics needs to be involved in preservation determinations. Additionally, a project, that performs a major regional function (such as transforming the edges of a river or a bay) can transcend other considerations and demand preservation simply for the life-enhancing qualities that it confers on a place. A unique example of a particular landscape type or environmental/ecological character (such as a wetland or bird habitat) also deserves to be preserved for the same reason. Finally, examples of different aesthetic periods also deserve to be preserved, for they are physical representations of a historical period in landscape design. Charles Birnbaum's book, *Preserving Modern Landscape Architecture*, provides a valuable study of this issue, particularly as it relates to modern landscape design. There are, however, other important periods and categories that must also be considered.

The problem of deciding what is valuable enough to be preserved within the modern whirlwind pace of change is daunting. A major part of the solution has to start with educating the public about the importance of designed landscapes. This education should begin at an early age and include the elements that form a critical eye for judgment of the values of environment and landscape design.

As with all art forms, there are a variety of opinions about what constitutes the essence of the art of landscape design. What differentiates our art is that it is multidimensional—based as it is on the physical experience of moving through the landscape. As we move, all of our senses are engaged: We become aware of colors, smells, sounds, and the feel of earth and stone underfoot. The emotional impact of water in pools, streams, and waterfalls tugs at us consciously and subconsciously. No other art form designs with so many elements of nature, with experiences that are often extremely ephemeral. The enjoyment of landscapes is primarily experiential. That is another reason why special critical judgment is needed to evaluate the worth of these designs and decide what should be preserved.

Some of my own experiences with preservation in the past few years have been excruciatingly painful. Much of this, of course, comes about because my practice has extended over a period of fifty-plus years. Things have changed a great deal over that period of time. Many of my early works in cities were designed for conditions that have been vastly modified. My work in the 1960s and 1970s was built during the urban-redevelopment period, when large swathes of "ghetto" areas were demolished. These early attempts to make major improvements in the environment of urban housing were considered mandatory at the time. Since then, of course, policy and approach have changed. Cities, streets, plazas, and parks, which were designed in revolutionary ways, are now under attack for not solving the requirements of modern downtowns with their emphasis on commercialism.

In the meantime, a number of my projects have been subjected to redesign. Usually, without my involvement in the redesign and rebuilding, their character and quality are changed forever. Some of this is actually being attempted as I write this essay. Usually, this process is not polite. In most cases I feel there is a great loss to the communities for which they were built. When people in these communities have asked for my involvement, the bureaucracies have often suggested that I "would be too busy" or "would resist any changes" or, worse, "wouldn't be interested."

To a certain extent I feel that things are changing for the better. More and more citizens have become interested in their environments and they want a stronger voice in their affairs. More and more people have become aware of the role that landscape design plays in their lives. In my own lifetime, understanding about our design profession has changed greatly, and its role as an art form is now appreciated.

Ultimately a great part of educating the public about landscape design lies in empowering people and making them aware of their civic role in planning and protecting their physical surroundings. This can be a heavy responsibility, but it can also be an expansive one. We have good role models to follow in the larger environmental movement. We can learn from them and interact with like-minded groups to bring attention to this need for thoughtful preservation of the best examples of this life-enhancing landscape art form.

Figure 3. The United Nations Plaza fountain in San Francisco under attack November 2003 (Andrew Sullivan)

Lawrence Halprin is a distinguished practitioner of landscape architecture and environmental planning. Born in 1916, he began his landscape architectural career with Thomas Church in San Francisco after completing his studies at Cornell University, the University of Wisconsin, and the Harvard Design School. He is one of the preeminent place-makers of the twentieth century. He is an ecologist, environmentalist, city planner, urban designer, architect, writer-theorist, and artist. His many honors include the 2002 Medal of Art award, the nation's highest honor for artistic excellence.

NOTES

This paper was prepared by Lawrence Halprin for the first edition of The Cultural Landscape Foundation's on-line newsletter, *Views & Vistas*. The CLF has made it available for this collection of essays.

Skyline Park: Preservation Ethics and Public Space

Mark W. Johnson

Figure 1. *The linear space of Denver's Skyline Park was terminated by the Daniels and Fisher Tower, the single historic building saved from urban renewal. (All photographs, Mark Johnson)*

Figure 2. *Halprin's concept recalled the canyons and waterfalls of the region.*

Context Skyline Park was built as the centerpiece of Denver's Skyline Urban Renewal District in the early 1970s. After demolition of an extensive neighborhood of traditional brick and cast-iron loft buildings, Skyline Park established a vision of urbanism that was current in the urban design of the times—the creation of urbane places for public retreat, the recall of nature through design abstraction, the establishment of new places for healthy public gathering, and the creation of a physical form that expressed a formal and sociological future that was unlike, even disconnected from, the past. Skyline Park was to be an antidote to the coldness of urban life and the romantic complement to a renewed, modern city.

In the 1950s Denver's leaders became concerned with the progressive neglect and decay of the older parts of downtown. Deterioration of businesses, buildings, and the social fabric was attributed to a number of causes, including the age, size, and design of structures (largely turn-of-the-century), the absence of new business investment, decaying infrastructure, inadequate auto access, and other factors. After a series of efforts by groups including the Urban Land Institute and the Downtown Denver Improvement Association and much discussion in the local press, the Denver Urban Renewal Commission (and later Authority) was formed to address these issues. In 1957 the commission published a report called Planning of the Central Area that proposed key ideas such as the development of a public park atop a large parking garage served by a new expressway linkage. Civic leaders believed that providing rapid access, parking, public space, and a pedestrian system elevated above the street would be critical to revitalization. Through a series of further plans, the idea of creating a three-block linear park was put forward. The park was envisioned as becoming a terminus to the traditional downtown on the southeast and the gateway to the renewal district on the northwest.

The firm of Baume, Polivnick and Hatami prepared a master plan for the Skyline district including urban-design guidelines for development and numerous variations of the proposed park. Lawrence Halprin was engaged to design Skyline Park as the primary public space of the district. His design appears to be derivative of earlier works in Portland, emphasizing sculpted, abstracted landscape forms, water features, and isolation from the adjacent street within a substantial forested enclosure. Entering the park brings you out of the city and into a complex of concrete canyons and bottomlands. Typical of Halprin's work, the design emphasizes linear movement along the three-block length of the project, punctuated by side canyons, sculptural events, and numerous sitting areas. Halprin and his firm prepared many alternatives of the park, all of

Figure 3. Aerial sketch of the proposed master plan for rebuilding the park, Design Workshop, 1997: This plan would have raised the sunken park to street level to increase pedestrian activity.

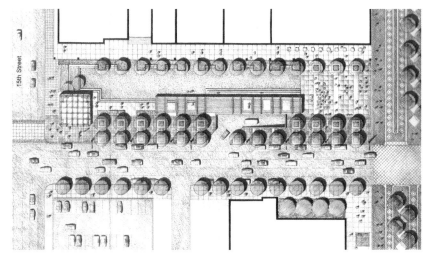

Figure 4. Proposed master plan indicating lawns, pavilions, and plazas for pedestrians, Design Workshop, 1997

which were predicated on the assumption that all three blocks of park would be built above parking. This led to a basic design concept that placed a line of high berms along the street edge of the park, providing soil depth for a continuous grove of trees. The park became a paved, walled enclave set down and back from the street, with a sequence of modulated spaces, sitting areas, sloping lawns, and one major water feature per block. A well-documented history of the park is available in *Denver's Skyline Park: A History* by Paul Foster and Barbara Gibson, published in 2001.

Skyline was built between roughly 1972 and 1975 in three phases that change subtly in design from block to block. The initial block, with the contemporary Park Central building, was achieved first. New buildings adjoining the remaining blocks took much longer to achieve. As much as twelve years went by before buildings enclosed the park. During this time some of the vision was forgotten: The final block includes a substantial length where the park frontage is parking garage.

When the park was opened it was a major public success, well attended and maintained. Over time, however, public use and maintenance levels declined. Physical and social deterioration set in. As the economy declined in the 1980s, downtown Denver lost a significant share of its retail base and struggled to achieve new housing, office, and entertainment uses. By the 1990s, however, these trends were turning, and a growing population of new downtown residents and office workers started to question the purpose and condition of the park.

By the mid 1990s the park was seen as an eyesore, an enclave for drug users and the homeless, and a bad influence on business and real estate values. The future of Skyline Park became an issue of discussion in public and private forums, especially in the 1995 Downtown Summit called by Mayor Wellington Webb to address the future of downtown. The Downtown Summit consisted of committee work and public discourse in an open forum of business leaders, property owners, policy makers, residents, and citizens in general. Skyline Park was a topic of considerable concern, as were the social issues associated with it.

In response to this, a local design firm held a pro bono student-intern charrette on the future of the park. The firm brought a group of landscape architecture students to the site and performed a review of the park's conditions and characteristics and further proposed a range of conceptual design responses. The charrette results were presented at a public meeting sponsored by the downtown business organization and attended by a cross section of the downtown community. The firm was then engaged by the City's Department of Parks and Recreation to prepare the *Skyline Park Master Plan*, published in 1997 with a preliminary

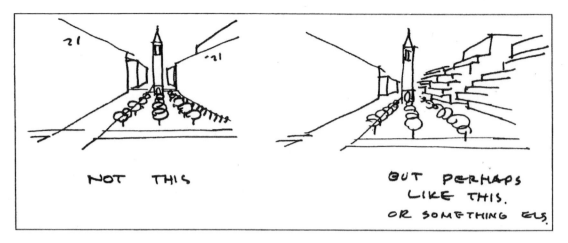

Figure 8. At the edge of the park along Arapahoe Street berms keep pedestrians from entering the park.

Figure 5. Halprin's sketch shows the original idea of terracing buildings on the west side of the park in order to open the park spatially and to the sun. Halprin Design Notes, 5/19/70

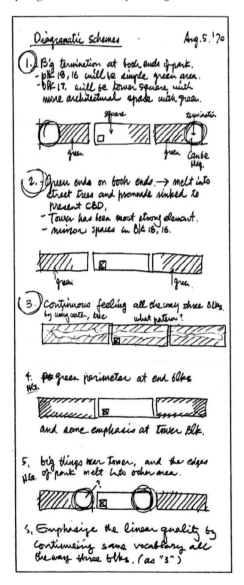

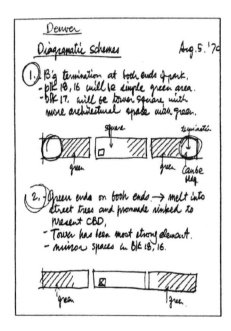

Figure 9. Sunken interior park spaces are intimate in scale, but subject to illicit activities.

Figure 7. Halprin's sketches study the merits of creating termination to the ends of the park or leaving the ends open and green. Halprin Design Notes, 5/19/70 (All sketches, courtesy of The Lawrence Halprin Collection, Architectural Archives, University of Pennsylvania)

Figure 10. The fountains have fallen into disrepair. Although people were originally supposed to engage with the water, climbing is now precluded.

Figure 6. Halprin's sketches explore the rhythm of open and closed spaces within the three-block park. Halprin Design Notes, 5/19/70

Figure 11. Open plaza spaces are sunken from street level. Berms along the street do not allow mid-block access or visibility into interior spaces.

Figure 12. The 16th Street Mall, with entry to Skyline Park on the right

Figure 13. Private fences added at the 16th Street entry to the park support cafes in summer but preclude pedestrians when not in use.

Figure 14. A portion of the park is fenced off for restaurant use. The overall lack of activity in the park led to the decision to allow eateries as a way of providing informal surveillance.

Inventory and Assessment published in 1996. The effort was well planned and performed with substantial dialogue and community process. The master plan calls for complete demolition of the existing park and replacement with a scheme that is a combination of plazas and promenade with lawns, shaded areas, an amphitheater, and importantly, replacement of the berms that hide the park from the street with perimeter walkways to improve real as well as perceived access and security issues. Although no capital funds were available for the improvements, the Parks and Recreation Department made substantial efforts to clean up the park and to improve maintenance, including the addition of flowers and shrubs and the interim repair of two of the three fountains. The conditions of the park improved due to these efforts as well as to increased police activity.

The master plan recommended that "a public/private management entity should be formed to plan, program, and manage a series of organized events" to supplement and expand the range of activities that would bring life to the park. This recommendation led to a further planning effort, managed jointly by the City and County of Denver and the Downtown Denver Partnership, a membership organization of private downtown interests that has played a leadership role in downtown issues for many years. The Skyline Park Revitalization Council was formed with broad representation and "with the goal of developing a new and dynamic vision for the park that will give it new life as a great public space in an active and vibrant downtown." This effort included additional analysis of the park with a series of council and public meetings to inform the recommendations, which were presented in the April 2001 report, entitled *Skyline Park Revitalization Initiative*. The report presents an extensive urban-design framework for the park within its context, emphasizing precedents from other places and recommending many specific ideas for active and passive uses of the park.

The *Revitalization Initiative* recommended demolition of the existing park and replacement with a highly adaptable, highly programmed, and highly managed assemblage of public spaces and venues for activity labeled the "DENVER EXPERIENCE." Elements such as performance spaces, a "Gazebo in the Garden," a skating rink, and street closures for special events were proposed. This plan reflects recent lessons from other cities that have experienced similar problems with urban spaces, notably Pioneer Square Park in Portland, Post Office Square in Boston, and Bryant Park in New York City. In each of these cases a partnership of public and private interests was created to provide a high level of programming and management—in each case with great success and acclaim. The *Revitalization Initiative* further recommended the selection of a designer to redesign the park to achieve its goals. A design team headed by Thomas Balsley Associates of New York was selected and is engaged in the design process at the time of this writing.

Question The Downtown Denver Partnership has taken a lead role in the planning of downtown since 1983 with the opening of the Sixteenth Street Mall and election of the visionary Federico Peña as mayor. By the late 1990s the Partnership had established a solid reputation of vision and implementation to improve downtown living, retail, infrastructure, and the public realm. Logically the Partnership entered and supported the dialogue regarding the condition and future of the park. In the year of 2000-2001 the Partnership reached a tentative agreement with the Denver Mayor's Office to lead an effort to create a new master plan for the park. As this effort developed into the selection process for designers, some preservation and design professionals in the community became concerned that preservation and adaptive-use options had not yet received adequate public dialogue.

It became clear that even though there had been a public process that explored the condition, management, and reuse of the park, not enough public interaction, dialogue, and reflection had occurred. A controversy emerged as to whether the process was open to further debate. To test this, a local firm proposed a symposium with the School of Architecture and Planning of the University of Colorado at Denver. Once the symposium was proposed publicly, additional concerned voices emerged, leading to a rethinking of the process by the Partnership and the Mayor's Office. As a result, the leadership of the new master plan shifted from the private sector to the City Department of Parks and Recreation, with the involvement of the Mayor's Office and the Downtown Denver Partnership. A Design Advisory Committee was established, Thomas Balsley Associates was engaged, and a new, open dialogue is under way, including a visit to Lawrence Halprin by a delegation from the Design Advisory Committee. This committee is broadly representative of business, preservation, and design voices, promising a favorable outcome through the application of a public process.

The question is this: What are the ethical issues and standards that should apply when evaluating an important landscape designed by a prominent figure?

The process described above in the evaluation and planning for the redevelopment of Skyline Park is not unique. In fact, it is typical. Concerned citizens, special interests including preservation groups, and city government undertook a lengthy, multistep effort to define the problems and to seek the best possible solution. They hired qualified,

intelligent professionals who led an open process. Yet controversy emerged and grew over the issues of preservation, adaptive use, or redesign of the park. Debates such as this are taking place around the country as cities address the aging of urban-renewal areas and their public spaces. The intent of this paper is to raise awareness of the ethical questions that should be addressed and ones that may be useful in establishing fair processes for guiding policy and decisions regarding important public places.

Response The primary conclusion to be drawn from the Skyline Park example is this: Virtually everyone involved, from professionals to policy makers to the public, looked at the park and its problems within a narrow slice of contemporary time. The park is called outdated, rigid, inflexible, deteriorated, dysfunctional, etcetera. Even the historical analysis presents the historical context and notes how that context continued to change during design and into today. This is, of course, true—because society and our ideas of culture continually change as economies, populations, media, and events impact our cultural responses. Culture changes, and the public's use, enjoyment, and veneration of public spaces changes accordingly. Most public spaces go through cycles of use and disuse over time, requiring, variously, efforts to revitalize them or efforts to manage overuse. Central Park in New York is probably the striking example of these cycles. But somehow in spite of the quality of people and process surrounding Skyline Park, there was a rush to judgment: The park was bad and needed replacement.

In reviewing the history of this recent process some conclusions bear mention.

Negativity A surprising negativity about the existing park pervades most of the documents produced in the process. Instead of an explanation of the history and purpose of the park, the very first documents label the park as having "problems." The inventory document begins each section by describing a problem—generally in one sentence—and then proposes solutions. The reader tends to conclude that the park is a compendium of problems. The idea of the park as a once-progressive solution within a new urban vision is never presented until the history was written in 2001.

Empirical Analysis The conclusions that were made regarding the conditions of the park were casual observations not based in empirical analysis of the actual park conditions or park use. There were no behavioral investigations; no measures taken as to the time, location, and nature of various activities or populations; and no analysis of what the causes were. The debate con-

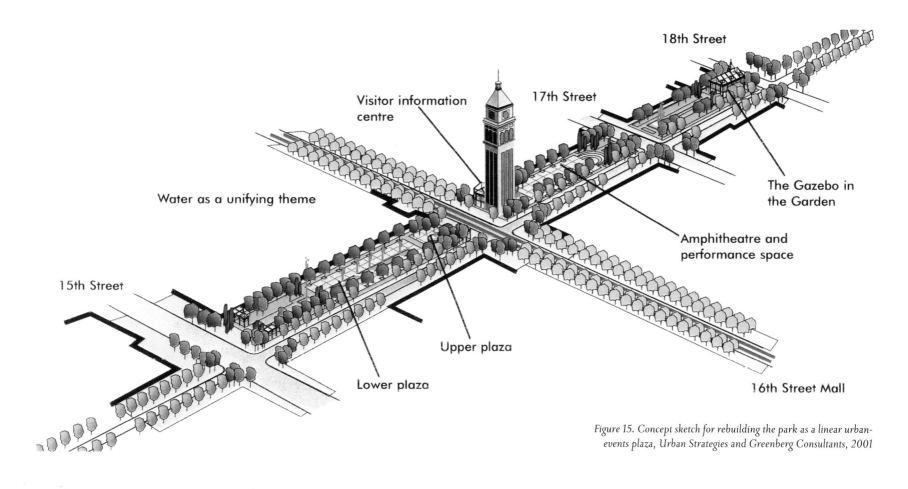

Figure 15. *Concept sketch for rebuilding the park as a linear urban-events plaza, Urban Strategies and Greenberg Consultants, 2001*

EXAMPLE OF VERTICAL USE AND ZONES OF ACTIVITIES

Figure 16. The original concept section shows vertical separation of vehicles, retail, office, and other uses. Skyline Urban Design and Development Study, 1968

tinues today about whether the problems of the park are those of design or management. In fact, they are almost certainly both. But without an empirical analysis of cause and effect, the arguments are based in speculation and supposition. This leads to debates of opinion over fact, controversy, and great difficulty in finding consensus, much less conclusion.

Design Integrity There has been much discussion of whether the park works for today and questions about whether the design is what the original designer intended, wanted, and so forth. Preservationists tend to call attention to the integrity of the physical design for its time and its current physical integrity. In fact, other than the fountain mechanical systems and plantings, Skyline Park is highly intact and in fine condition. Those who favor redesign call attention to the lack of integrity in the

design, citing the changed cultural conditions, the progress and changed character of downtown, and the rigid character of an original design that could not easily adapt to the culture. To them, integrity would include adaptability to changing times. In their view the design has only physical integrity, not conceptual integrity. The park is seen as a single-minded solution to one problem, a solution applicable at one point in time.

Precedent The professionals who prepared the plans focused on precedents from other cities in the United States and Europe, including photographs of other famous places as examples of good public space. Just as their analysis of the existing conditions of the park failed to explain the empirical relationship between form and function, so do their references to other successful places lack explanation. There is a

47

strong tendency in the reports to observe the physical characteristics of other places and to assume that these are the reasons that the places are successful. The professionals have missed the essential linkage between the cultures of each place and the reason that the physical forms of the places resonate with and satisfy those cultures.

Program The program proposals in the reports are not empirical or the result of investigation of Denver or downtown activities, events, venues, or needs. The park and its current uses or potential uses are not fitted into an explanation of the context of social venues that Skyline Park might supplement. Instead, the programmatic elements of the reports are advocacy statements by the professionals, apparently based in professional experience in other places. This is not wrong. Professionals should bring their experience to bear. However, in the absence of a clear understanding of what role this park could and should play in downtown life, the program is conjecture.

Temporality It is not just the culture that changes with time. We as humans have a tendency to assume that we have learned from history and that our current view of things is adequate. In this process, people looked at the park as an artifact of another time, a time that is no longer relevant. It is easy to question and even to scoff at the ideas and assumptions of the urban-renewal period. Razing whole blocks of cities for freeways, isolating tall buildings with no relationship to streets, forgetting the importance of streets in city life, along with many other ideas, were the basis for urban-renewal visions around the country. We tend to look back today and assume that those people were somehow misguided or lacked an understanding of the city. Therefore we tend to disregard the artifacts that were left behind.

The Skyline Park process suffered from the very same mind-set that existed during urban renewal. The planners at that time looked around at other precedents of decay and renewal and sought out the very best minds of the time. They used the most current theories of city-building and studied the problem in great detail and with many alternatives. They questioned themselves, made their best judgments, and built Skyline Park. The planners of the current Skyline Park revitalization effort have engaged in at least some of the same thinking. Judging the park as an artifact of another time, they have focused on contemporary theories and successes, borrowed those lessons, and applied them to this park. This is the corollary to the lack of an empirical analysis. We are in danger of repeating the mistakes of the past, albeit with more knowledge but perhaps not with sufficient rigor.

Process The documentation of the history of Skyline Park was not completed until 2001, five years after the debate and planning effort began. The failure to understand the historic issues of the park at the outset appears to have had a surprising effect: Public and professional opinion was developed and even matured toward demolition and replacement as a result of the process. When the process itself was questioned, it was defended primarily on the grounds that it had been very open, iterative, and lengthy. These are good reasons to defend a process, but in this case it was one that was launched and executed in advance of basic fact-finding. In this context, the debate became polarized.

Ethics The Skyline Park example raises a number of questions of an ethical nature. Perhaps if they are raised here other efforts may be able to ask them in advance, avoiding some of the problems. Each group in the process can be questioned about its attitude or approach.

Design Professionals: The design professionals in this process made no unusual assumptions. But the result of their assumptions did influence the process.

The act of providing design services pro bono with students may have influenced opinions about the park. The professionals may have underestimated the impact that this effort would have—not on the design outcome, but on public opinion. Is it possible that the fact that a firm was willing to offer free services to address a problem actually validated the existence and magnitude of the problem in the public's mind?

The rush to judge the park against precedents without empirical analysis of the functional/behavioral issues of the park itself reinforces opinion, not fact. Would opinion have been different if the professionals had done this analysis? The failure to educate the public on the essential linkage of place, culture, and time in precedents and analysis allows for opinions to be both shallow and divergent. More important, doesn't the absence of this step put more emphasis on the design professionals' opinion?

Design professionals commonly complain that the public does not respect their opinions as deeply as the professionals would like. In this case it appears that the design professionals' opinions in fact had a substantial impact on public opinion, for reasons cited above. Did the professionals' rush to judgment by comparing the place to precedents create an effectively self-referencing argument?

Business Community: The business community experiences the failure of public space directly in terms of lost revenue and lost value. They also experience value cycles for a variety of reasons that are unrelated to public space, such as the quality of their own business efforts and the marketplace. Did the business community find a convenient scapegoat for other economic problems in the social problems of the park?

Did the business community assume that it was the private sector's role to define the best purposes and uses of public space, and in so doing, was the process sufficiently balanced for all constituents?

Did the business community focus on short-term problem-solving when the existence of public space is fundamentally a long-term value?

Preservation Community: The preservation community participated at various levels throughout the Skyline process, yet controversy over preservation erupted anyway.

Would the process have been different if the preservation community had created a positive understanding of the history of the park and its place in history? How would this have been funded?

Would the process have been informed and logical if the preservation community had established and advocated principles for review of historic properties? Would it be possible for these principles to be imposed on a city process that is not linked to the official landmark-designation process?

The preservation community has not yet embraced landscapes, much less modern designed landscapes, as valuable places and artifacts. Will the Skyline process lead to a stronger conviction of the worth of such landscapes?

Policy Makers: The policy makers were placed in a reactive mode in this process after the public and the business community insisted that there was a problem that needed to be solved.

By leading a process that focused on replacing the park, did policy makers undermine their responsibility to the long-term health of the city?

By partnering with the business community, and effectively delegating public authority over public space, did the policy makers create a condition where the opinions about public space would be overly influenced by the benefits to the private sector?

Conclusion A public symposium dedicated to Skyline Park was held as part of the final design process by Thomas Balsley Associates. The symposium included presentations of the history of the park, a history of Lawrence Halprin and the work of his firm, a history of modernism in landscape and urban renewal, and discussion of the roles of public and private sectors in the design and use of public space. A constructive dialogue began among all the parties, contributing more information to the design process.

Since that time, the Design Advisory Committee has reviewed numerous design alternatives for the park. A day-long work session with Lawrence Halprin created a park-modification proposal that Halprin was willing to endorse. This scheme was acceptable to some members of the committee but unacceptable to others, spurring the development of numerous alternatives. As of this writing, a compromise scheme has emerged that includes a general redesign of the park with the retention of numerous individual elements of the Halprin design. The Design Advisory Committee has completed its work, and a smaller review committee has been established to continue to review progress as the design develops. Many opinions have been presented in public forums, but no clear consensus of support has emerged for the recommended scheme itself.

Regardless of the viability of the many modern urban landscapes that exist in American cities, spaces such as Skyline Park were the embodiment of a high order of urbanistic thinking and ideals by the greatest talents of the time. The themes of city-building, healthy societies, and vibrant economies are embedded in the forms of these unique places. Whether they are worthy of preservation is a question that may take time to answer. They deserve, however, investigation, analysis, and judgment within their own time, our time, and that future time we cannot predict. When we look at the great cities of the world we always find layer upon layer of time represented in the urban landscape. Perhaps that is a clue about how we should preserve, modify, and rebuild these urban legacies.

Mark Johnson, FASLA, is a founding principal of Civitas in Denver, Colorado, and a frequent lecturer on the use and design of public space. His projects focus on the relationship of nature and landscape in the urban condition, with an emphasis on the public role in setting an agenda for design.

Case Study: Manhattan Square Park, Rochester, New York

Ken Smith

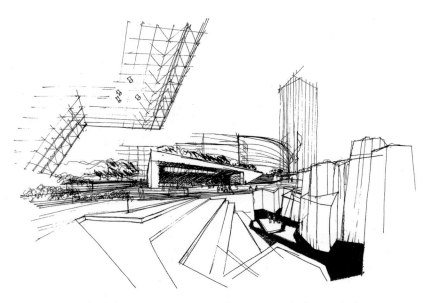

Figure 1. Design sketch for Manhattan Square, Rochester, New York, showing the fountain plaza area (All sketches, Jack Gaffney, Lawrence Halprin & Associates)

There is something particularly troubling about the thirty-year mark for a landscape architecture project: just old enough to show wear of material and design ideology, past its initial acclaim and success, but not yet reassessed by historians for its merit as part of a larger and more enduring critical assessment. Such works force us to confront many difficult questions.

Today the works of Lawrence Halprin are particularly threatened with alteration and destruction. Perhaps his best-known works in California, Washington State, and Oregon are the safest and best protected. His lesser-known works in other parts of the country are the most vulnerable. Nicollet Mall was destroyed a decade ago. Skyline Park in Denver, Colorado, the Virginia Museum sculpture garden in Richmond, Virginia, and Manhattan Square Park in Rochester, New York, are currently threatened.

The design community is only now beginning to reassess the work of the early postmodern-era including Halprin's seminal work with Charles Moore at Sea Ranch and Halprin's subsequent urban projects. A more complete assessment of the work of this period and Halprin's work in particular will begin to build a stronger case for its preservation. A number of misconceptions exist relative to Halprin's work that are partly responsible for the relative lack of support for its preservation. In the following discussion I would like to address some of these common misconceptions and perhaps construct a more sympathetic interpretation of Halprin's design legacy.

The first misconception, one rooted in today's New Urbanism, is that Halprin's design work represented a radical break from the American park tradition. On the contrary, Halprin played a pivotal mid-century role in revitalizing and transforming the American tradition of parks as established by Frederick Law Olmsted. Halprin drew upon Olmsted's belief that the American park should use the power of nature as a humanizing element in the city. Olmsted believed the park should have an apart-ness from the city where citizens could go for respite. One of Olmsted's fundamental innovations was the use of grade separation to functionally separate pedestrian and vehicular uses and orchestrate spatial sequence as he did successfully at Central Park in Manhattan and Prospect Park in Brooklyn. Halprin's own practice of drawing on nature for design ideas and forms, as demonstrated in seminal projects like Forecourt Fountain and Lovejoy Plaza in Portland, Oregon, falls soundly within this American tradition, as does his use of dramatic grade change to create spaces that have an essential separateness from the surrounding city and its traffic.

As Halprin states in the issue of *Process Architecture* (1978) devoted to his work:

I start by going back to nature. For instance I always show the source of water. Here it starts slow, and then runs and runs. Sounds and lights and gurgles and splashes are all part of my intentions. It is not just to look good; it includes all the sensory perceptions. And there are different levels: This is one event where the water comes down and you can come around behind it. Here is that idea of experiential equivalent: You see this happen in nature.... You can have the same experience man-made, but it is not copied.

Another misconception about Halprin's work involves the issue of contextualism. A common criticism is that his parks and urban landscapes are not contextual, that they are separated from the street, and that the grade changes cut the spaces off from public life. A cursory review of Halprin's designs for Manhattan Square Park reveals an interesting contextualism. When the Halprin design is overlaid on the pre-urban-renewal historic street pattern for the neighborhood several features of the park take on significance in their alignments and design form. What today may seem to be an arbitrary forty-five-degree alignment within the

Figure 2. Design sketch of fountain and space-frame features

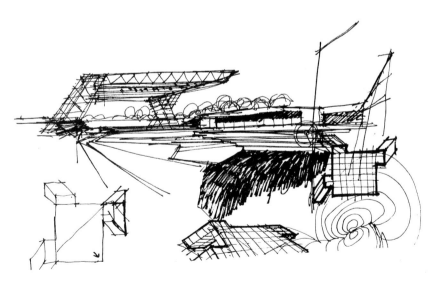

Figure 3. Sketch of space frame

Figure 4. Sketch of the allée-like promenade

park's design is actually based upon the dominant orientation of the former historic street pattern of the area, namely McNerney Street and Broadway. The other major park feature, Halprin's promenade, is oriented on axis with the historic George Street alignment. Halprin was also concerned with local context as revealed in his use of the park design to recall the topography and dramatic falls and grade changes of the Genesee River in Rochester. There is a strong parallel between going down into Halprin's Fountain Plaza and going down into the River Gorge that runs through the City of Rochester. These contextualizing alignments make formal connections between the new park and the historic fabric of the city and its immediate neighborhood.

A third misconception is that times have changed and that the social ideas and experiments from the 1960s and 1970s are not relevant today. Pertinent to this discussion are Halprin's ideas about the social functions of an urban park. In *Cities* (New York: Reinhold Publishing, 1963) Halprin writes,

> The life of cities is of two kinds—one is public and social, extroverted and interrelated. It is the life of the streets and plazas, the great parks and civic spaces and the dense activity and excitement of the shopping areas. This life is mostly out in the open in the great urban spaces, where crowds gather and people participate in the exciting urban relationships which they seek as social beings.

Halprin continues:

> There is, too, a second kind of life in the city—private and introverted, the personal, individual, self-oriented life which seeks quiet and seclusion and privacy. This private life has need for open spaces of a different kind. . . . It needs enclosure and quiet, removed from crowds and a quality of calm and relaxation. The city should respond to both needs and both kinds of activity for they are equally important parts of the urban environment we are seeking.

Halprin's social vision for public open space and parks is borne out in the rather remarkable program listing for Manhattan Square Park, which was itemized on a presentation plan from the Halprin office. These program notes confirm the social intention of the park in providing spaces for social activity, group activity, and programmed events as well as quieter and more introspective spaces with a remarkable list

Figure 5. Manhattan Square Park fountain plaza, view from the space frame (John Zeltri, 1975)

Figure 6. Manhattan Square Park fountain plaza (John Zeltri, 1975)

of forty-one activities ranging from kite flying to rendezvous to lunch and basketball.

Halprin's park in Rochester, New York, was begun in early 1971 and completed in 1976. Documents in the Halprin Archive at the University of Pennsylvania include a contract dated 1971, undated design sketches showing evolution of the park design (Figures 1–4), design development documents dated 15 December 1971, and construction documents dated 20 November 1972. There is also construction-observation correspondence, including punch-list items dated March 1976, all authored by Tim Wilson, who was a principal in Halprin's New York City office.

The New York office oversaw the project with a lot of working back and forth with the San Francisco office, according to Wilson, who

Figure 7. Manhattan Square Park fountain plaza fountain (John Zeltri, 1975)

Figure 8. Manhattan Square Park space frame (Tim Wilson, 1975)

Figure 9. Manhattan Square Park amphitheater steps at the fountain plaza area (John Zeltri, 1975)

Figure 10. Manhattan Square Park ice-skating pavilion (Tim Wilson, 1975).

made available original photographs of the completed project and provided access to a published schematic-design booklet not included in the Halprin Archive. Manhattan Square Park was part of a large urban-renewal program for Rochester's downtown. The park was intended to be the centerpiece of a high-rise development of housing and offices adjacent to the downtown core. The park was completed, but only one of the planned residential towers surrounding the park was ever built.

The park design contains a number of signature elements and a few surprisingly original features. Among the familiar elements drawn from Halprin's mature style are the fountain feature, which bears strong similarity to Halprin's Lovejoy and Auditorium Forecourt fountains, and the

berm garden, which is reminiscent of Halprin's Pettigrove Park in Portland. Among the elements without direct precedent are the soaring space frame and observation tower that hovers over the sunken plaza. The park also contained a children's play area, a promenade, and an ice-skating rink and pavilion (Figures 5–10).

The park was much acclaimed upon its completion. Period photographs show the park full of people, and first-person accounts indicate that the park originally had a level of activity programming and social events that contributed to its use and popularity. *Architectural Record* commented in November 1975 that the park had a "plaza-fountain similar to—but larger than—Halprin's Lovejoy Plaza in Portland," pouring 30 million gallons of water per day into an amphitheater sunken below

Figure 12. Current view of park from Court Street (Mark Reid, 2001)

Figure 11. Current park conditions in berm area with mature trees (Mark Reid, Design Strategies, Inc., 2001)

Figure 13. Current view of park, children's play area, without the original play features (Mark Reid, 2001)

street level. The description continues: "This together with one of the largest flat space frames ever built forms a spectacular introduction to the remaining park, designed for relatively unstructured activities, . . . an introduction to the park's more pastoral pleasures." The article also comments on the innovative use of the fountain's water as a cooling tower for the refrigeration system of the ice-skating rink.

A description of Manhattan Square Park in the 1978 *Process Architecture* captures the essence of the work:

> Forms are drawn from nature but are abstracted in a man-made way. . . . This park is the most multipurpose facility Halprin has ever designed for a downtown area. What was added here is a fourth dimension, for this project takes this idea of the plaza with all of its uses and extends it upward. This creates additional usable space on other levels, amidst a huge space frame. . . . The traditional plaza has been extended below ground also. . . and reasserts Halprin's sentiments regarding the separation of vehicular and pedestrian worlds.

The space frame functioned in several important ways. First, it served as an important element highly visible several blocks away from the park. It also served as a kind of proscenium, framing the theatrical space of the sunken fountain plaza, which was intended to serve as a large and organic amphitheater. The space frame was originally outfitted with park lighting and a sound system. The other significant use was as an overlook tower rising from the structure and allowing open views across the park and downtown cityscape.

At Manhattan Square Park Halprin created some remarkable spatial sequences, vertical juxtapositions, and dramatic shifts of scale. Most obvious are the dramatic fountain plaza and the space frame. The informal plantings and bermed landforms afford intimate spatial enclosure and shade as a counterpart to the open fountain and plaza area. The tunnel entrance and enclosed space of the children's play area is evocative and memorable. Maintenance facilities are ingeniously tucked underneath berms so that they are simultaneously accessible and out of sight.

The park suffered budget cuts in operations and programming in the 1980s, and the fountain feature has not been operated for a number of years. Today the children's playground is devoid of its original play features, and some park plantings have been removed. The open pavilion at the ice rink has been badly altered. The pavilion's openings have been blocked off resulting in a dark and oppressive space. The City still programs the park on a limited basis for ice-skating and special-events concerts (Figures 11–13).

In 2001 a study was conducted to determine the future of the park. During focus-group meetings with residents and stakeholders there was no noticeable groundswell of support for either preservation or wholesale redesign of the park. Most people didn't understand the park and the ideas that formed its original design. While many people had fond memories of the park when the fountain was still functioning, most people admitted that they don't use the park today. Because the observation tower has been closed for many years and the lighting system on the space frame has not been maintained, many people also questioned the purpose of the space frame. The present condition of the park with its nonfunctioning fountain and general deterioration makes it hard to appreciate and unattractive for use.

Even with the park's many problems, an engineering assessment in 2001 found that the park's retaining walls, fountain, and space frame to be all structurally sound. There has been some surface deterioration of the walls, the fountain mechanical system needs a substantial upgrade, and the space frame needs to be painted. The ice-skating rink's cooling system is still functioning but will need to be replaced in the near future. In general the electrical system is deteriorated and inadequate.

In spite of material deterioration, changing tastes and appreciation, and lack of park programming the park still retains its signature qualities. The strong spatial structure of the park is still evident and powerful. While the sunken public spaces are not fashionable in current design practice, the grade changes create a great degree of spatial diversity. They are signature elements in the park's design, contextually related to the falls landscape of the Genesee River Valley. Today the park is in need of restoration and improvement. The strength of the park's original design, overall quality of the original construction, and intact condition of most of its original features merit its preservation and restoration.

Ken Smith, a New York City-based landscape architect, focuses his practice on projects that explore the symbolic content and expressive power of landscape as an art form. Current projects include the Lever House, Harlem Gateway, and East River Ferry Piers.

APPENDIX A
Contents of the Halprin Collection

The Halprin Archive is a remarkable resource for historical and restoration design research. The Halprin Collection includes the following materials related to Manhattan Square Park.

1. Undated set of ten perspective sketches. These sketches are assumed to have preceded the design-development document set dated 15 December 1971. This remarkable set of design sketches illustrates the early evolution of the park design concepts and intentions.

2. Mylar set of original design development documents dated 15 December 1971, prepared by the Lawrence Halprin and Associates. This set includes the following sheets:
Drawing 1. Site Plan, Layout and Planting Plan 1"=20'
Drawing 2. Grading Plan and Utility Plan 1"=20'
Drawing 3. Plaza, Fountain Detail Plan 1"=20'
Drawing 4. Plaza, Fountain Detail Sections 1"=20'
Drawing 5. Architectural Details
Drawing 6. Landscape Details
Drawing 7. Space Frame Plan and Elevations
Drawing 8. Structural Details

3. Presentation Print. This print of the 15 December 1971 Drawing 1 has been hand-shadowed and contains a hand-stenciled listing of park program notes.

4. Pencil on Vellum sections of the park, dated 14 March 1972. These detailed scale studies of the grade changes at the fountain area occurred mid-way between design development and working drawings.

5. Pencil on Vellum "Section A," no date. This detailed section of the fountain area and landform grading of the meadow area is assumed to have been done about the same time as the fountain sections described above.

6. Undated and unbound blueprint set of detailed drawings, some with title blocks

partially cut off. The drawings in this set include:
Drawing SF1. Space Frame Framing Plans
Drawing SF2. Space Frame Framing Plans
Drawing SF3. Foundation Plan and Details (with redline mark-up)
Drawing SF4. Details and Sections (marked "Preliminary Not For Construction")
Drawing SF5. Stair Section and Details (noted in red "Incomplete")
Irrigation Plan by George W. Bell of Milbrae, California, drawn on Halprin's Layout Plan. (fountain planters marked with red X, noting no irrigation in plan)

7. Working Drawings, dated 20 November 1972. This partial set of final documents bear the New York City address on the title block and are signed and sealed by Lawrence Halprin, State of New York Landscape Architect #0454, and James Timothy Wilson, Registered Architect State of New York #011325. These drawings include:
Drawing L.1. Layout Plan 1"=20'
Drawing L.2. Material Plan + Detail Key 1"-20'
Drawing L.4. Planting Plan 1"=20'
Drawing L.5. Fountain / Plaza 1/8"=1'-0" (rendered print)
Drawing L.6. Fountain / Plaza Grading and Drainage Plan 1/8" = 1'-0"
Drawing L.7. Fountain / Plaza Grid 1/4"=1'-0"
Drawing L.8. Multi-Purpose Space (ice-warming house)
Drawing L.9. Multi-Purpose Space (restaurant)
Drawing L.10 Play Area + Spray Pool

8. The other materials in the archive are correspondence files. It is interesting to note that there are no files pertaining to the design phase of the project, only the contract documents, fee documents, and correspondence related to construction observation. The construction-observation correspondence in the files was authored by Tim Wilson of the New York City office. Job lists in the archive confirm that this was a New York office job (number 1071). No design-related files are known to have survived.

Church, Eckbo, Halprin, and the Modern Urban Landscape

Marc Treib

The history of modern landscape architecture in California has been told primarily in terms of the garden, and it was in the garden that many of the ideas by which modernism has been known were first tested.[1] Modern urban landscape design was less easily proposed and perceived, and to a large degree it evolved from initial efforts in the design of gardens and suburban academic and corporate campuses. This essay covers a short period of time, roughly the twenty years between 1948 and 1968, when California landscape architects moved from the residential to the urban arena, at first applying suburban manners to this new public context. In time, however, particularly in the works of Lawrence Halprin for New York City, ideas more strictly rooted in the urban situation evolved, with a gradual merging of landscape and urban-design practice.

The icon of the modern garden is, of course, the Donnell garden, designed by Thomas Church with Lawrence Halprin and George Rockrise and first completed in 1948.[2] That this relatively small garden on the Sonoma hills north of San Francisco Bay became the poster child for the new trend was no accident. At the end of World War II Church was the preeminent modern landscape architect in California—if not nationally—and his notoriety increased significantly in the postwar years.[3] His work was published regionally in the *San Francisco Chronicle* and *Sunset* magazine, and later nationally in *House Beautiful*. For its editor Elizabeth Gordon, champion of Frank Lloyd Wright and things American, Church fit a very much needed niche: innovative yet not austere, proposing but also accepting, with an idiom that swung from the highly biomorphic and abstract to the assertively classical.[4]

That Gordon would have continued to champion Church had he continued in such an extreme mode is doubtful. But in many ways the Donnell project marked the apogee of Church's modernist swing, matched possibly only by the Martin garden in Aptos from almost the same year. More appealing to *House Beautiful*'s editorship was Church's continued focus on privacy, use, and people evidenced by the Donnell project's concern with living outdoors in the grand tradition of the California myth. The pool garden and its attendant structures, in fact, were built before the house itself, having been accepted by the local authorities as a useful water reservoir even when wartime restrictions limited the use of certain building materials. Its spaces were nonaxial and its look was not "natural," that is, not "natural" in the English-landscape-garden-tradition sense of the term. Ten years before, the neophyte landscape architect Garrett Eckbo had asserted that "arbitrary station points and axial vistas are no solution of the problem," and in this project Church and company seemed to agree.[5] The Donnell garden also used California modernism for its architecture—the lanai and guesthouse

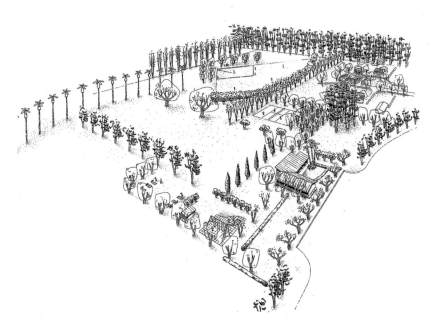

Figure 1. Park and Community Building, Farm Security Administration Camp, Harlington, Texas, 1940, perspective, Garrett Eckbo/FSA (Drawing by Carlos Dinaz)

Figure 2. Donnell garden, Somona, California, 1948–1952, Thomas Church (Marc Treib, 1999)

were designed by George Rockrise working in the Church office. And its vocabulary, with its seemingly free forms and angular play, smacked of everything contemporary, everything new, everything optimistic after the close of nearly four years of total war.

From 1946 until 1952 Church's office produced an impressive number of garden schemes, a high percentage of which were realized. They featured grand gestures and sweeping curves, often playing the angle against the zigzag. While in some ways they seem to share a manner similar to those of Roberto Burle Marx, Church's gardens were based on a more social base and a different spatial construct, and they never relied on horticultural specificity to the same degree as those of the Brazilian landscape architect.[6] But there were always those gardens in Church's production that were more traditional in aspect, that employed none of this newfangled vocabulary. Common to all of them, however, were Church's oft-repeated dictum that gardens are for people

and his concern for the life within the landscape rather than its composition as an abstraction or invention or horticultural specialization for its own sake.[7] This period, when Halprin, Rockrise, and June Meehan comprised the Church staff, neatly mixed just the right personalities and talents at just the right time: when clients as well as the designers shared a willingness to tackle the new.

Landscape history tends to acknowledge Church's gardens from the 1940s and 1950s and little else. Early in his career, however, Church designed one of his few urban landscapes: the 1936 entry court for San Francisco's War Memorial Opera House. This project reveals how classically oriented Church had remained until the end of the decade when interests in the new design ideas and, to a lesser extent, new art forms began to influence his vocabulary. This resistance to new formal ideas was especially true of the few public projects where the classical remained influential. Not improbably his association with architect

Figure 3. Union Bank Plaza, Los Angeles, California, 1968, Eckbo, Dean, Austin, Williams (Garrett Eckbo, 1978)

William Wilson Wurster and their meeting with Alvar Aalto in Helsinki in 1937 also nudged Church along a more modernist trajectory. In time there were larger projects, including wartime workers housing in Vallejo, the extensive housing development at Park Merced in San Francisco (1939-1952), and the mid-1950s General Motors Technical Center, whose architect Eero Saarinen had selected Church as consultant. Dan Kiley tells that Eero Saarinen had wanted to work with him to get the commission—he knew him from their time shared working in Washington—but that he was still in service in Europe. He suggested Church and Kiley's Harvard classmate Garrett Eckbo. Church was the obviously senior figure and this probably appealed to the General Motors people. The nature of the Californian's contribution has been difficult to ascertain, however, for the scheme appears to be pure Saarinen. The few existing drawings are the product of the Detroit landscape architect Edward A. Eichstedt.[8] While his designs for gardens were immediately identifiable, there is little sense of a Church landscape at larger scale or one that addresses the particular conditions of the city.

One senses that Church conceived the greater landscape as a conglomerate of private gardens that congealed, in some way, to create a greater entity. His decades' long work on the University of California, Berkeley, and Stanford University campuses produced volumes of planting and terraces but little design of exceptional quality. Again, these interventions read as discrete interventions and adjustments to exiting conditions taken one or two at a time, rather than as a sweeping vision of the campus landscape as a whole. One suspects that Church also considered society in just this way: The community was a conglomerate of individuals banded together to forge the greater entity. In this view he contrasted rigorously with Garrett Eckbo, his junior by about half a generation.

Eckbo also studied at the University of California, graduating in the midst of the Depression.[9] But Eckbo was more socially inclined, and

winning a scholarship through competition, he went to Harvard for graduate study—as Church had before him. At Harvard Eckbo found himself at odds with the existing landscape power structure and the strong remnants of the more codified Beaux Arts tradition. He bristled at the dicta of Hubbard and Kimball's *Introduction to the Study of Landscape Design*, writing marginal comments such as "Why must the designer 'choose character.' Why can't that develop naturally?"[10] Instead, he drifted toward the architecture program in general and Walter Gropius in particular. While he enjoyed the newness of International Style architecture—particularly Mies van der Rohe's Barcelona Pavilion—it was Gropius's social ideas that were the truly formative aspect of Eckbo's education at Harvard.

A comparison of Church's and Eckbo's respective thesis topics reveals the differences in their attitudes toward landscape architecture and society. (Note, however, that these are student works and that at least a decade separates the two theses.) In 1927, after returning from a year of travel in Europe under a Sheldon Fellowship, Church submitted his thesis: "A Study of Mediterranean Gardens and Their Adaptability to California Conditions." Here he was concerned with climate, topographic manipulation, vernacular forms, and horticultural practice. Eckbo's thesis, in contrast, proposed "Contempoville" as an exploration of the new suburb in which each resident occupied his or her own piece of land, but shared a common space with the local community center.

Figure 4. Fulton Street Mall, Fresno, California, 1965, Eckbo, Dean, Austin, Williams with Victor Gruen Associates (Garrett Eckbo, 1968)

Figure 5. Fulton Street Mall, Fresno, California, 1965, Eckbo, Dean, Austin, Williams with Victor Gruen Associates (Garrett Eckbo, 1968)

The parts always led to the whole; the landscape provided the matrix.[11]

Quite indicatively, Eckbo's first long-term employment for the Farm Security Administration on the staff of the Western Regional Office was serving the migrant agricultural workers. Thwarting the dual devastating effects of the Dust Bowl and exploitative labor management, the FSA created a series of camps that also served as safe havens—so vividly described in John Steinbeck's *Grapes of Wrath*. Social service was a mission for the young Eckbo, and it was here—perhaps ironically, or quixotically—that some of the most advanced ideas in landscape architecture were implemented, albeit in a simplified and abstracted form. The lessons learned at Harvard centered on defining interrelated spaces through the vegetal planting of hedges and windbreaks. This approach informed the design of several of the camps in California's Central Valley and in Texas. There was little in the traditional Beaux Arts teaching that addressed problems such as these, that is, problems by which landscape could confront most directly the problems encountered when creating landscapes for living. One had to be modern to address such conditions and to advance any viable solutions.

Throughout the 1940s Eckbo engaged in active practice with Robert Royston and Edward Williams in the Bay Area and, after 1946, in Los Angeles. The gardens that issued from this practice intensified the effects of Church's lighter hand, with spaces of increased paving, bounded sites, imaginatively-shaped swimming pools, and what he termed (as had Christopher Tunnard before him) the "sculptural" use of plants.[12] His doctrine, distilled from fifteen years of thinking and practice, appeared in 1950 as the important treatise *Landscapes for Living*—still the preeminent formulation of comprehensive ideas for landscape architecture in the twentieth century. In that book, Eckbo spoke of city planning as "the great creative work of the great future, that magnificent art of the human environment toward which all three space-planning professions gravitate

automatically in the course of their work."[13] There was a "ladder," he believed, that linked "site planning through neighborhood, town, city, and regional planning to national planning," and the linkages could be planned at every stage.[14] He believed, as well, in the use of "some sort of spatial relations, rhythmic or continuous, which tends to fuse them into larger-scale units which have a scale relation to the form of the hills." By these means—through design—"the contradictions between development and site can be resolved and result in greater quality than their mere accumulation produced." Eckbo cautions, however, that "this overall pattern [does not] have to regiment the individual or subvert democracy, as some may say."[15]

These quotations suggest that the urban situation posed something of a dilemma to this generation of landscape designers. The majority of ideas proposed by Church and Eckbo focused on the suburban condition even when applied to community development.[16] From the 1940s, and into the 1960s, these were the prime spheres for residential development. How would the new landscape architecture influence the postwar building boom or the downtowns instigated by the rapidly expanding urban periphery? The rise of the automobile begat the growth of the regional shopping center championed by architect and planner Victor Gruen, which begat a consequential decay of the shopping areas in the Central City.[17] In time the downtown could hardly compete—either with the volume discounts and acres of parking afforded by the more

Figure 6. Nicollet Mall, Minneapolis, Minnesota, 1967, Lawrence Halprin (Marc Treib, 1976)

Figure 7. Fulton Street Mall, Fresno, California, 1965, Eckbo, Dean, Austin, Williams with Victor Gruen Associates (Garrett Eckbo, 1987)

conveniently positioned shopping centers or with the demographic shifts that placed more residents outside the center. Could landscape architecture mitigate the effects of this trend and help lure the consumer back to the downtown? The answer seemed to lie in the pedestrianizing of the urban street, essentially proposing that if the shopping mall would not come to the downtown, the downtown could become a shopping mall.

Of course, landscape architects had designed plazas for office buildings and cultural centers throughout the country; certainly by the end of the 1950s and early 1960s it was a common landscape type. Eckbo's most outstanding effort in this genre—in form, if not in exact typology—was the 1968 Union Bank Plaza in Los Angeles. Essentially a roof garden, like Osmundson and Staley's celebrated 1960 roof garden for the Kaiser Center in Oakland, the Union Bank's grids of shade trees and swoopy forms conspired to create a world opposing the rectangular confines of the site and its support structure. Coral and jacaranda trees bloomed in vivid red or pale lavender, and the pools and trees are still regarded as an oasis destination by the bank's employees and those of surrounding

buildings. In many ways, however, the plaza was less an urban space than a corporate garden for its employees and for others who might climb the heights necessary to reach it. The plaza level is raised from the street to provide levels of parking below.

In that regard, the 1965 Fulton Street Mall in Fresno was a far more ambitious proposal for an innovative model. Having been designed for the car, Fulton Street challenged the designer to bring its width into greater accord with pedestrian movement and its length into comprehensibility and continued delight. The solution, for the designers Victor Gruen and Associates with Eckbo, Dean & Williams, seems to lie with block-by-block development relying on plantings as buffers and features and on water elements for flow and animation. Sculpture by Alexander Calder, Peter Voulkos, Jan de Swart, and Claire Falkenstein completed the design palette and provided focal points of visual interest. In this particular instance the solution proved to be popular—at least in the early years—but a good measure of that success was attributed to the sufficient parking in proximity to the mall. Business success could not be the product of new landscape design ideas alone, however, and one project alone does not seem to have been sufficient to bring the requisite numbers of people to the area—or it was at first sufficient, but not over the long run.

Throughout his life, the Fulton Street Mall remained one of Eckbo's favorite projects and the one of which he was most proud. In 1986, he wrote about revisiting the site after almost twenty years. Yes, he admitted, a number of the shops were vacant and boarded, but before the mall was constructed fully a third of the shops were vacant—a far greater percentage than in 1986. In Eckbo's eyes the trees had matured but on the whole maintenance had been rather good. Some water features had been converted to planters, par for the course with public designs. Eckbo noted: "Despite the city's unstated goal to attract white middle-class shoppers from beyond downtown, the only whites were a few male indigents. People, mostly Blacks and Latinos of all ages—relaxing, shopping, and enjoying themselves—gave the mall a lively feeling." "Success of a mall," he observes, should "be judged by the movement and mood of its participants."[18] On those terms, he found the design vital.

The next generation of planners and designers built upon these first tentative efforts at revitalizing the downtown through the new pedestrianized street. After Church, Lawrence Halprin emerged as the most vibrant figure on the Bay Area—and later national and international—landscape scenes. Halprin began his career with a series of handsome gardens that furthered the insights developed for his projects while working in the Church office, but early on he began to display visions of greater spheres of interest, with an ambition to match. Almost contemporaneously with the project in Fresno was the 1967 Nicollet Mall project in downtown Minneapolis. Here the total banishment of vehicular traffic was thwarted by introducing a meandering traffic lane for buses, effectively vivifying—at least to a limited degree—the project's ten-block length. Planting and custom lighting were the most identifiable of the design elements, but like many later mall projects, Nicollet also relied to a great degree on the nature of its paving. In retrospect, Halprin reflected on his intentions for the Nicollet design: "To encourage pedestrian movement, the wide and curving streetscape is designed to offer places to sit, with graphics, sculpture, fountains, and various plantings of trees and flowers along the way."[19] His sketchbooks indicate that he sought out solutions for winter as well as summer use, investigating the possibilities for using radiant heating, for example, to encourage prolonged occupation.[20] A 1976 Minnesota architecture guide concluded its entry with this observation: "The Nicollet Mall is generally conceded to be one of the most successful malls in the country. This is owing in part to the way it has been closely related to new construction and the revamping of existing buildings, to the elevated skyways across adjoining streets, and to the fact that the linear nature of Nicollet still retains some motor traffic."[21]

Like the Fresno Mall, however, time and administration have been unkind to Nicollet Mall in a somewhat familiar story. The issue has been equally a question of economic viability and the social composition of the users as well as management, maintenance, and refurbishing. Tom Martinson, a planner based in Edina and coauthor of the Minnesota architecture guide, summarized the situation in this way:

> As a piece, [the mall design] was terrific, what you might call an "organic" design because it all seemed to work together and was in effect much more than the sum of its individual elements. However, the mall had its enemies, particularly the City's Public Works Department who think of Minneapolis as their domain and didn't like the idea of the planning department and business community deciding on this Californian, who was ipso facto a weirdo by virtue of his residence. Public Works seemed to do as little as possible to maintain the mall and took great delight when some of the mosaics eventually popped up. They convinced the City Council that outsiders could never understand the relationship of climate to public works and thus pressed to handle an expansion of the mall all by themselves. This in and of itself was a bad idea—there was a certain rightness to it ending at

Ghirardelli Square, San Francisco, California, 1965, Lawrence Halprin with Wurster, Bernardi and Emmons (Marc Treib, 1987)

> Tenth Street—but about 1980 I/- Public Works expanded the mall about four blocks south to Grant Street. It was embarrassingly mediocre, even for something designed by civil engineers, and fortunately the City decided to revamp the mall with actual designers just a few years later—a nice way of doing away with the Public Works Department mall.

Martinson reports that by his evaluation nothing really remains of the Halprin design.[22]

The Nicollet Mall project also fed on the earlier 1965 Halprin design for Ghirardelli Square in San Francisco, designed in collaboration with architects Wurster Bernardi and Emmons. This project was a landmark adaptive use of a nineteenth-century structure once used for the production of chocolate and one that set a national trend for festive retail in revamped industrial buildings. In conceiving the design, Halprin imagined the upper plaza as a "beehive of excitement," essentially conflating the market with the civic plaza—another prescient gesture. Preserving much, but not all, of the old brick structure, the plaza developed over three levels of parking, using "layers of shops" to ease the flow of movement from top to bottom and vice versa. In early sketches trees surrounding a fountain are thoughtfully spaced and pruned to allow views of the Bay. Addressing Beach Street, Halprin suggested setting back the lowest block thirty feet to allow for an allée of horse chestnuts to create a "handsome promenade."[23] The landscape linked the various levels with a play of spaces of varying openness and sunlight; nighttime illumination provided a play of brilliants, recalling the night lighting at the Tivoli Gardens in Copenhagen. Protection from the wind was paramount.

The overall tone of the Ghirardelli Square design was decidedly soft, avoiding any extreme statements of modernism and instead looking toward the past for an appropriate tone. It also proposed a model for a

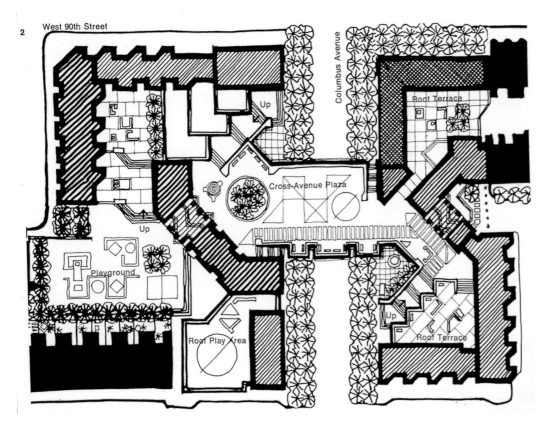

West 90th Street

Columbus Avenue

Up

Roof Terrace

Cross-Avenue Plaza

Up

Playground

Up

Roof Play Area

Roof Terrace

Figure 9. Westside Renewal Area, Cross-Avenue Plaza Plan, from New York New York, *1968, Lawrence Halprin*

greater whole: "I . . . think this is a demonstration of what a whole city could do, if you could imagine it ten times bigger," stated the landscape architect.[24] In Halprin's writing, however, he is less interested in the structure than in its use, less in the theater than in the play: "space as theater," as he termed it.[25]

In retrospect, we might look at these projects as overly optimistic, grounded in the idea that the design of a landscape can sufficiently counter, if not totally vanquish, the forces of economics and demographics. But there is also something curiously suburban in many of these designs in and of themselves, as if the elements of the residential garden had been adopted and adapted to a linear public space. Each block becomes a garden animated by pedestrians and the flow of water up and outward. Greenery structures the spaces and reduces the scale while screening the adjacent shops; flowers accent the increments with color and dabs of fragrance. Perhaps this is the implicit message of these public spaces (a somewhat new typology): If we can make the public space a garden, people will experience pleasure and transfer it to consumption. Like the regional shopping mall itself, the street becomes the garden, but a garden for a broader population rather than for just a single family.

In the mid-1960s Halprin was commissioned by New York's Housing and Development Commission to study six districts in the city selected through their joint counsel. The landscape architect had been directed to study the open space, vegetation, and street furniture in these urban districts; instead he broadened his purview to a considerable extent and examined life quality as a whole. In the preface to the book, *New York New York*, the 1968 publication that resulted from the study, Halprin explained how each set of factors—open space, architectural, social, climatic, visual, and political—were all inextricably interlocked; any viable proposals for this area must be necessarily broad. Thus, he worked with a team of consultants beyond the architects, landscape architects, and planners in his own office, adding to their knowledge and skills those of Gestalt psychologists, sociologists, and anthropologists. In the book Halprin reads the sites sympathetically, perhaps due to his having been born in the Bronx and raised in Brooklyn. Indeed, Halprin refers to himself as a "renegade New Yorker" living in the San Francisco Bay Area, but retaining New York sympathies.

A review of the book and its design proposals somewhat stymies any preconception one might have had based on a review of Halprin's landscape projects to that time. His early gardens introduced some extremely mannered formal play—the early Caygill garden in Orinda, for example—or imaginative recastings from historical models, such as the McIntyre garden in Los Gatos from 1961 with its almost Alhambran layout and details. On the other hand, Halprin had also designed the landscape for Marquis and Stoller's highly successful St. Francis Square in the Western Addition redevelopment district in San Francisco. This project, paired with his work on Vernon DeMars's Easter Hill Village in Richmond, demonstrates Halprin's competence in planning appropriate landscapes for housing far beyond those of the private suburban garden.[26]

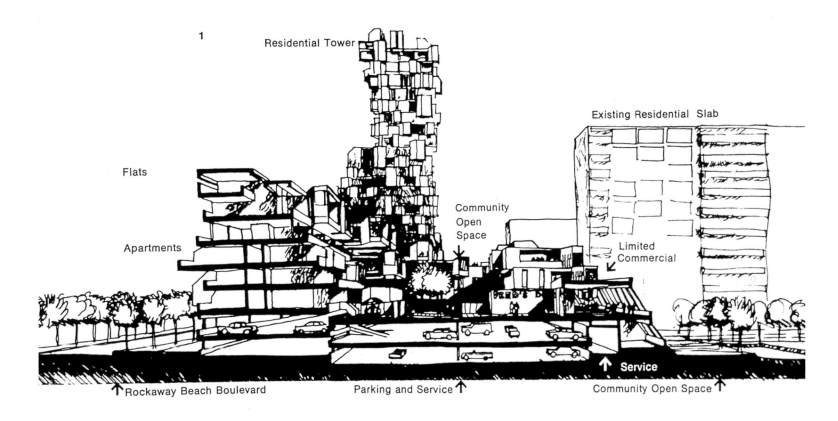

1

Residential Tower

Existing Residential Slab

Flats

Community
Open
Space

Limited
Commercial

Apartments

Service

Rockaway Beach Boulevard

Parking and Service

Community Open Space

Figure 10. Dayton Towers, Multidimensional Structure, section, from New York New York, *1968, Lawrence Halprin*

Perhaps it is not too far-fetched to relate Halprin's *New York, New York* to Camillo Sitte's *Art of Building Cities* of 1889.[27] In that classic study Sitte railed against the overly open spaces that accompanied the recasting of the former Viennese fortifications into the peripheral artery known as the Ringstrasse. Sitte was horrified by the gargantuan governmental palaces set on their spatially-undefined sites, effectively destroying all that was urban and good in historical city-building. In reaction, he studied landmark open spaces in the medieval northern European city, focusing on the Rathaus and the church as the punctuations to the undistinguished masses of urban buildings. In a similar manner Halprin's proposal requests greater construction, noting that only if the open space is defined and related to living patterns can it achieve viability and vitality. The model of the Le Corbusian tower in the park, by which so much redevelopment had been marked, was clearly unsuccessful—if not an unmitigated disaster—in cities throughout the developed world. Here Halprin suggests ideas previously proffered in his own books *Cities* (1963, revised edition 1972) and *Freeways* (1966).[28] The fitting out of these spaces is left remarkably undeveloped. He cites trees or walls and little else in greater specificity. Surprisingly, there is virtually no sense of the detail proposed in such books as Gordon Cullen's *Townscape* or even the careful descriptions in Halprin's own volumes on cities.[29]

For the West Side renewal, for example, the design calls for perimeter construction to more fully enclose communal gardens; neighboring brownstone occupants might even join together to create a common mews among them, with entrances turned toward this inner space. Columbus Avenue would be flanked by twin allées of trees to buffer the facades of the buildings and to grant a unity to the grand sweep of the avenue. An elevated plaza bridging the street breaks this linear flow and removes pedestrian movement from vehicular traffic: a strategy Halprin developed to its extreme in the later Seattle Freeway Park. Here in New York the gesture is interesting, if tentative, but one questions the resultant quality of life on the street beneath the plaza.[30] The over-the-road link is a popular element in Halprin's New York proposals; it attempts to join neighborhood units into larger conglomerates to achieve greater social viability through numbers. Given the later success of the Seattle Freeway Park, the landscape architect's fascination with this element is understandable, but it hardly seems that it could have been a panacea for the problems of the Manhattan neighborhood in the 1960s. Still, that was then and this is now, and hindsight is nearly always 20/20.

Only in the Tompkins Square area does the report accept construction more or less as given, directing its attention primarily to the spaces between the existing buildings. We see linkages created by rows of trees and shrubs, play areas and roof gardens, and even an indoor swimming pool. Interestingly, one quadrant of the site is left purposely undeveloped, the report noting that its use should be determined only in consultation with the neighborhood.

The authors argue throughout for complexity, or more specifically, "complexification": "Complexity, rather than simplicity, is a major factor in the process of making cities exciting and interesting and therefore satisfying places to live."[31] They take issue with much of the then-existing redevelopment strategies as providing blocks and spaces that are too large, too open, and too impersonal. By the time of the report, the cracks had already appeared on the surface of urban-renewal policy, and studies such as Jane Jacobs's celebrated *The Death and Life of Great American Cities* from 1961 had set the ideological stage for the theater that Halprin then designed.[32] The greater question remains as to how well the proposal addressed these social issues head-on.

New York New York is a sympathetic look at six areas of the city, investigating, studying, and designing for increased livability (a word that also entered the design vocabulary about that time). Unusually for a landscape architect, there is little in the study concerning landscape architecture itself, that is, if we restrict the idea of landscape architecture to vegetation, water, paving materials and patterns. Halprin and company assumed a much greater role in the making of cities, operating more in the manner of urban designers than traditional landscape architects. In this they reflected the broadened vision and interdisciplinary activities of the various design professions evolving during the 1960s.

Little of the rich proposal of 1968 was ever implemented, and one wonders about the vagaries of governmental policies, agencies, and personalities and their effect on the making of livable cities. But as a document of its period—a document that traces the increased influence of landscape architecture in the urban sphere—the *New York New York* study is an important work. More than half the book concerns general topics ranging from psychology (admittedly of the more pop variety) to population density and microclimates. These were so broadly sketched that they probably had little actual value other than to raise the issue as one of design concern. (The climate issues, for example, are almost entirely adapted from Victor Olgyay's classic *Design with Climate*.)[33] The strategies and schemes themselves are essentially graphic and verbal guidelines, frustratingly vague in their development as design. While there is little with which to argue, there is little upon which we could build directly—other than elements like the over-the-road deck and some street planting. But regardless of these drawbacks, one sees here how the adopted Californian, or renegade New Yorker, Lawrence Halprin had successfully moved from the arena of the suburban West Coast garden to the densest of East Coast cities—and the potential influence that such a scheme could have exerted had it been given sufficient political backing and funding.

In some ways this displacement was prophetic for a profession seeking its own definition, with increased recognition and credibility among the general public. The era of the garden as the flagship of the landscape architect had passed, and the move from suburbia to the city as the primary arena was under way. Interestingly, when the second icon of modern landscape design appeared almost twenty years after the realization of the Donnell garden, it was an urban park designed by a New York firm and built in New York. That icon, of course, was Zion and Breen's 1964 design for Paley Park. But that's another story.[34]

Mark Treib is a professor of architecture at the University of California, Berkeley. He has written extensively on modern architecture and landscape architecture. His most recent book is The Architecture of Landscape, 1940–1960 *(Philadelphia: University of Pennsylvania Press, 2002). Thomas Church, Landscape Architect will appear in Fall 2003.*

NOTES

1 See Marc Treib, "Axioms for a Modern Landscape Architecture," in Marc Treib, ed., *Modern Landscape Architecture: A Critical Review* (Cambridge: The MIT Press, 1993), pp. 38–67.

2 One says "first completed" because the Donnell landscape was realized in sections, with the pool area occupied late 1948, the lanai (living pavilion) in 1949, and the house and its garden about two years later.

3 Peter Shepheard included the Donnell garden (as well as Church's Martin garden in Aptos) in *Modern Gardens* (London: The Architectural Press, 1953), the first postwar English survey of the new landscape design, pp. 42–47. It was inexplicably missing in one of the succeeding landmark studies, Susan and Geoffrey Jellicoe's *Modern Private Gardens* (London: Abelard-Schuman, 1968). Presumably, by that date—some twenty years after its completion—the Donnell project was no longer new, despite the fact that the modernity of its design was far greater than that of most of the gar-dens included in the book. In *Modern Gardens in the Landscape* (New York: Museum of Modern Art, 1964) Elizabeth Kassler notes, "Related neither to buildings or to land form, most swimming pools are literally for swimmers only. This pool is an exception. Its shape was inspired by the winding creeks of salt marshes seen through the frame of live oaks. The large landscape is expanded, not denied," p. 69.

4 See Dianne Harris, "Making Your Private World: Modern Landscape Architecture and House Beautiful, 1945-1965," in Marc Treib, ed., *The Architecture of Landscape, 1940–1960* (Philadelphia: University of Pennsylvania Press, 2002), pp. 180–205.

5 Space, in Eckbo's mind, was paramount: "More important than the enumeration of specific functions is the development of three-dimensional volumes of outdoor space, to pleasantly environ these willfully and unpredictably motile beings." He added that "the basic aim should be recreation," in F.A. Mercer, ed., *Gardens and Gardening* (London: The Studio, 1939), p. 19.

6 Although Church and Burle Marx shared an affinity for both the curve and the checkerboard and at first appear to evoke considerable parallels, there were several basic differences to their respective approaches. For one, Church read the site and developed ideas thereafter; Burle Marx often painted a plan inspired by the site conditions but not necessarily wed to them. In addition, Burle Marx exploited his vast horticultural knowledge, showcasing exotic plants, floral color, and leaf forms. Church was almost always more restrained and conservative in his plant selections and used them as building blocks rather than as ornament alone. Representative books on Burle Marx include P.M. Bardi, *The Tropical Gardens of Burle Marx* (New York: Reinhold Publishing, 1964); Giulio G. Rizzo, *Roberto Burle Marx: Il giardino del Novecento* (Florence: Catini & C, 1992); and William Adams, *Roberto Burle Marx: The Unnatural Art of the Garden* (New York: Museum of Modern Art, 1991).

7 Church's first book proclaimed just that belief: *Gardens Are for People* (New York: Reinhold Publishing, 1955).

8 See Edward A. Eichstedt, "Landscape at the General Motors Technical Center," *Landscape Architecture*, April 1952, 164–67.

9 After graduation in 1936 Eckbo headed south to Los Angeles to work for Armstrong Nurseries for about a year, by his tally completing about one hundred gardens. Most of these projects were executed in a California almost-modern comfortable-living style, and most of them featured abundant varieties of plants. See Marc Treib and Dorothée Imbert, *Garrett Eckbo: Modern Landscapes for Living* (Berkeley: University of California Press, 1997).

10 Henry Hubbard and Theodora Kimball, *An Introduction to the Study of Landscape Design* (New York: Macmillan Company, 1917), Eckbo marginalia, p. 73.

11 Eckbo's thesis refuted, in part, the isolated propositions for urban gardens published in his "Small Gardens in the City" project (*Pencil Points*, September 1937), although these did lay out and test the elements of a formal vocabulary he would mine for the rest of his career.

12 Christopher Tunnard, in the first real manifesto for modernism in landscape design, writes, "By far the widest field for symbolic representation is provided by living plant materials. As an ornament near water, what could be more expressive and complementary than the weeping willow? . . . Even the geometrical shapes of topiary, when presented in unconventional arrangements, will be seen to have acquired a meaning apart from their associations with the past," *Gardens in the Modern Landscape* (London: The Architectural Press, 1938), p. 102. Eckbo echoed his sentiments in *Landscape for Living* (New York: Duell, Sloan & Pearce, 1950): "Planting is seldom isolated, and then only by choice. It is an art of continuity, real or potential, by contrast with the art of entity which structural or refined design is." He continues, "Plant material, as an aggregation of units of unlimited variety and form, size, color, and texture, has esthetic possibilities which have scarcely been scratched," p. 95.

13 Ibid., p. 242.

14 Ibid.

15 Ibid.

16 It should be noted that Eckbo, with James Rose and Dan Kiley, as early as 1939 coauthored a series of articles that addressed the broad sweep of landscapes from the "primeval" to the urban. See Garrett Eckbo, Daniel U. Kiley, and James Rose, "Landscape Design in the Urban Environment," *Architectural Record*, May 1939, 70–77; "Landscape Design in the Rural Environment," *Architectural Record*, August 1939, 68–74; "Landscape Design in the Primeval Environment," *Architectural Record*, February 1940, 74–79.

17 See Victor Gruen, *Shopping Towns USA: The Planning of Shopping Centers* (New York: Reinhold Publishing, 1960) and *The Heart of Our Cities: The Urban Crisis: Diagnosis and Cure* (New York: Simon and Schuster, 1967).

18 Garrett Eckbo, "Fresno Mall Revisited," *Landscape Architecture*, November-December 1986, 54.

19 Lynne Creighton Neall, ed., *Lawrence Halprin: Changing Places* (San Francisco: San Francisco Museum of Modern Art, 1986), p. 127.

20 Chang, Ching-Yu, ed., *Lawrence Halprin, Process Architecture*, (1978) 1984, 121.

21 David Gebhard and Tom Martinson, *A Guide to the Architecture of Minnesota* (Minneapolis: University of Minnesota Press, 1976), p. 29.

22 E-mail, Tom Martinson to author, 17 February 2002.

23 *Lawrence Halprin, Notebooks 1959–1971* (Cambridge: The MIT Press, 1972), pp. 75–77.

24 Lawrence Halprin, *Process Architecture*, 106.

25 Neall, *Lawrence Halprin: Changing Places*, p. 126.

26 See Clare C. Cooper, *Easter Hill Village: Social Implications of Design* (New York: Free Press, 1975).

27 Camillo Sitte, trans. Charles Stuart, *The Art of Building Cities* (1945; reprint Westport, Connecticut: Hyperion Press, 1979); and George R. Collins and Christiane Crasemann Collins, *Camillo Sitte: The Birth of Modern Town Planning* (New York: Rizzoli International, 1986).

28 See Lawrence Halprin, *Cities* (1963; New York: Reinhold Publishing, 1966); and Lawrence Halprin, *Freeways* (New York: Reinhold Publishing, 1966).

29 Gordon Cullen, *Townscape* (London: The Architectural Press, 1971).

30 While it is somewhat unfair, one wonders what such places would be like by today's standards and how they would be retrofitted to meet current handicap requirements.

31 Lawrence Halprin & Associates, *New York New York* (New York: Department of Housing and Urban Development, 1968), p. 107.

32 Jane Jacobs, *The Death and Life of Great American Cities* (New York: Random House, 1961).

33 Victor Olgyay, *Design with Climate: Bioclimatic Approach to Architectural Regionalism* (Princeton: Princeton University Press, 1963).

34 That story would certainly feature the work of New York landscape architect M. Paul Friedberg, whose fruitful career has centered on the problems of the city and its people. See *M. Paul Friedberg: Landscape Design, Process Architecture*, 1989.

Preserving Modern Architecture and Landscape Architecture in Columbus, Indiana

Meg Storrow and John Kinsella

Figure 1. In 1942 First Christian Church was the origin of the Columbus experiment in modern architecture. (All photographs, Storrow & Kinsella)

In 1997–1998 Columbus, Indiana, a town noted for its collection of twentieth-century modern architecture, was experiencing angst within its architectural and historic preservation constituencies. First Christian Church, the earliest and perhaps the finest example of the city's dazzling array of world-class architecture, was planning to construct an addition that some felt would seriously compromise its status as a modernist icon. This 1942 church, designed by Eliel Saarinen, marked the beginning of a program of patronage for modern architecture that put this small midwestern town on the national cultural map.

In a visit to Columbus, sponsored by Historic Landmarks Foundation of Indiana and the Columbus historic preservation group Preserve to Enjoy, Carolyn Pitts of the National Park Service proposed that the modern architecture of Columbus be recognized through a National Historic Landmark nomination. Preserve to Enjoy, unique among such groups in that it understands the historic significance of modern architecture, grabbed the idea. They saw an opportunity to raise the consciousness of such stewards as the First Christian Church congregation as well as to enhance the prestige of the town's rich modernist heritage.

Preserve to Enjoy, with assistance from Historic Landmarks Foundation, commissioned our firm, Storrow Kinsella Associates, a landscape architecture firm, to prepare a National Register of Historic Places multiple-property documentation and individual National Historic Landmark nominations. The result would be the first multiple-property listing for modern architecture that included landscape architecture, specifically the work of Dan Kiley.

We assembled a team that included a historic preservation expert, an urban designer, and a landscape architect, from our staff, with assistance from a local Columbus architect and a Ball State University landscape architecture professor, all intimately familiar with Columbus modernist architecture as well as landscape architecture. As landscape architects, we felt compelled to recognize the multidisciplinary context of the subject architecture. As we reexamined the already familiar work it became even more obvious that the landscape architecture component was much more than the enhancement of individual sites in service to architecture. The perceived presence and sense of place of the overall compositions and of the townscape itself derived largely from the seamless integration of structure and setting, one of the tenets of modernism in the built environment. In consultation with the client group and Carolyn Pitts of the National Park Service, we therefore expanded the original scope of the project to include a complete consideration of landscape architecture and the allied design arts as a multiple property nomination for Modernism in Architecture, Landscape Architecture, Design, and Art.

Figure 2. Irwin Union Bank and its later addition, both architectural masterpieces, are connected by Dan Kiley's site design.

Figure 3. An allée of London plane trees by Dan Kiley created a park setting for two Cummins Engine facilities.

The narrative developed an overall view of the community and the forces that caused the significant works to be built. It established the framework of modern architecture and landscape architecture history within which the designers and their work in Columbus is represented. Two themes emerged and were identified as the basis for the multiple-property nomination: one, Modern Architecture and Landscape Architecture and, two, Patronage in Public Architecture.

National Historic Landmarks are preferably identified through theme studies, which are effective because they provide a comparative analysis of properties associated with a specific area of American history, for example the fur trade, earliest Americans, women's history, Greek Revival architecture, or labor history. In order to make the case for national significance, a theme study must provide the necessary national historic context so that national significance can be judged for a number of related properties.

The themes were developed as a way to explain the evolution of Columbus and Bartholomew County as a center for modern architecture. Two categories of associative property types were established to support theme development. The first, "Public Buildings, Structures, and Sites 1957–1965," was based on associative characteristics and the time period for the context of the Patronage in Public Architecture theme. While the time period was narrowed to 1957–1965, the foundation for future nominations was established by noting that the patronage program continues to support notable structures and landscapes. The second category of associative property types, "Buildings, Sites, and Structures Representing Modern Architecture and Landscape Architecture 1942–1965," was based on physical attributes and the time period for the context of the Modern Architecture and Landscape Architecture theme.

The patronage program for support of modern public architecture originated with the vision of J. Irwin Miller, then CEO of the Cummins Engine Company, a Columbus-based diesel-engine manufacturer and the town's major employer. He related in a 1981 interview with James Michener that the idea for the program originated in a discussion with architect Eero Saarinen, who described what was then a State Department policy of hiring leading American architects to design United States embassies. (Saarinen had designed those in Oslo and London.) Miller acknowledged that he initiated a similar program for Columbus largely for the good of his company, reasoning that good public architecture, particularly for schools, encouraged the attraction and retention of a quality workforce through the incentive of a quality environment. It was an early manifestation of the economic development/quality-of-life linkage and as such has widely influenced attitudes about corporate responsibility toward community development.

The Cummins Engine Foundation, the charitable arm of the corporation, established a program to pay the design fees for local public projects if the client group selected the design from a list developed by an independent panel of experts. The patronage program started more than thirty years ago, and since then many public resources have been constructed. In addition, the patronage program fostered an outstanding design sensibility in the community, resulting in private-sector construction of additional modern architecture resources. This was an interesting exercise for the landscape architecture component because we were able to show the evolution from landscape architecture relating to individual site development to what it is today, including public sites and the connective fabric that establishes the town character as a unified whole.

Since 1942 more than sixty structures and numerous other resources have been designed by the country's leading practitioners in architec-

Figure 4. Kiley's honey locust allée, viewed over the shoulder of the Henry Moore sculpture in the Miller garden

Figure 5. Kiley's processional, through hedge-defined parking courts, frames the First Christian Church spire.

ture, landscape architecture, and urban design. The result has been an extraordinary representation of mid-to-late twentieth-century design. The works are integrated into the community as schools, factories, office buildings, churches, government buildings, parks, bridges, houses, and gardens. The effort grew out of a very pragmatic response to the needs of a rapidly growing community and an embracing of the modernist tenets of form/function and problem-solving.

The Columbus area has a collection of modern buildings, landscapes, and public sculpture that reflects the development of these design idioms on a national basis. Many of the designers experimented with concepts and forms in Columbus that they then applied to larger, more clearly identifiable signature works elsewhere. These cultural resources reflect the design trends of the period in which they were constructed in response to a programmed quest for excellence in design and creative problem-solving. There is a broad crosssection of designers represented, rather than a collection of works by a small group.

The second phase of the project was to identify and prepare nominations for six resources to be nominated as National Historic Landmarks:

First Christian Church First Christian Church (1942) is one of the first modern religious buildings in the United States and an outstanding example of the work of Eliel Saarinen. The building was nationally recognized at the time of its construction. It had an impact on church design in the United States in the post-World War II era. First Christian Church is also important as the first modern building in Columbus. It illustrates Eliel Saarinen's genius in building composition and urban design. The integration of arts and crafts into both interior and exterior reflect the concept of total design that Saarinen had developed in his Finnish period and refined during his establishment and leadership of the Cranbrook

Academy collective of artisans in Bloomfield Hills, Michigan. The relationship of the building and the site's open space and the manner in which the total work relates to the surrounding urban fabric remain as lessons to later generations of designers.

Irwin Union Bank and Trust The Irwin Union Bank and Trust (1954) is a highly innovative bank design and an outstanding example of classic modernist form, a minimal but entirely functional glass pavilion referenced as Miesian in homage to the Mies van der Rohe Barcelona Pavilion. The work of Eliel Saarinen's son Eero Saarinen, Irwin Union Bank and Trust was possibly the first financial institution in the United States with glass walls and an open plan, dramatically differing from past solutions for banks and influencing the future of bank design. The Dan Kiley landscape of a tree-bosque surround is an extension of the building's formalism and a precursor to the structuralism he developed throughout his career. This property is one of a number of examples in Columbus, Indiana, that illustrate trends in modern architecture and landscape architecture. Its development coincided with that of the much larger and better-known General Motors Technical Center, a major influence in corporate architecture for years to come.

Miller House One of a small number of residences designed by Eero Saarinen, the Miller House (1957) is an important residential representation of the International Style, a subtype of the modern movement. Its design is informed by the Irwin Union Bank and Trust building in its formalism and refinement of detail. The landscape by Dan Kiley is one of the most important integrated modern designs in residential landscape architecture. Building and landscape are fully integrated in this collaboration, with a series of exterior roomlike spaces extending the pinwheel

Figure 6. McDowell School pavilions within an understated grove of London planes influenced by Kiley's earlier design

Figure 7. First Baptist Church sits on a promontory approached by Kiley's sequentially framed views.

organization of the principal structure. The gardens are such an icon of modernism that despite the owner's meticulous stewardship and mainte-nance of Kiley's composition, minor expressions of personal taste are the subject of debate within the design community.

North Christian Church Completed in 1964, North Christian Church is the work of architect Eero Saarinen with landscape architecture by Dan Kiley. This innovative design incorporates many aspects of modern archi-tectural interpretation of religious spaces and traditions. The landscape of the church represents the fusion of modern architecture and land-scape architecture. Kiley's planting organization perfectly complements and grounds the building in an expression of intense collaboration between architect and landscape architect. This was Eero Saarinen's last work, with its development assisted by members of Saarinen's studio who have achieved prominence on their own, including Kevin Roche, John Dinkeloo, and Paul Kennon, as well as John Kinsella, one of the coau-thors of this National Landmark theme study.

Mabel McDowell Elementary School Mabel McDowell Elementary School (1960) is an excellent representation of the effort in Columbus to improve the quality of life through outstanding design. The building is an early example of modern architecture in Columbus and an example of the con-textual work of John Carl Warnecke, a leading architect of the twentieth century. The site contains five separate one-story buildings linked by land-scaped courtyards and covered walkways. Four classroom buildings flank the central hub, which contains the cafeteria and administration spaces.

First Baptist Church First Baptist Church (1965) is an outstanding repre-sentation of the work of a distinguished American architect, Harry Mohr

Weese. It is generally thought to be his best work in Columbus, Indiana, where he completed numerous works of modern architecture. The design fees for this structure were paid through a privately sponsored program with the goal of improving the quality of life in Columbus by increasing the quality of its architectural environment, a mission inspired by the Cummins Engine Foundation's successful program.

The National Landmark nominations for Columbus have elevated the community's appreciation of the national significance of its modernist building and landscape architectural heritage. The nominations have also given the community new tools with which to engage the sometimes unknowing would-be perpetrators of damaging and devaluing change to these remarkable resources.

While the First Christian Church addition has proceeded, albeit in a way that sincerely attempts to pay homage to the original design, a State highway project that would have carved into the North Christian Church site has been redesigned for a lessened impact because of the protection afforded by the nomination.

But most rewarding to the authors of the study, as landscape architects, was the opportunity to gain recognition for the modernist landscape architecture of Columbus, to highlight its importance to the modernist movement, and, perhaps, to fashion a model for recognition of that importance elsewhere.

Meg Storrow and John W. Kinsella are principals with Storrow Kinsella Associates, a firm located in Indianapolis, Indiana, and based on its principals' disciplines of landscape architecture and urban design.

Dan Kiley: Planting on the Grid

Gregg Bleam

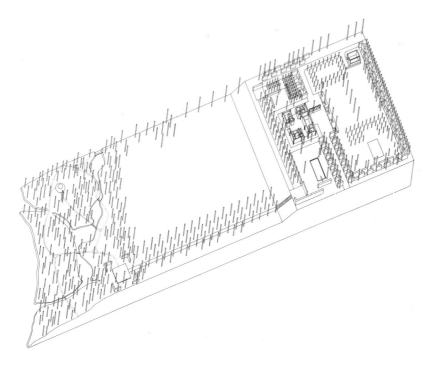

Figure 1. Miller garden, axonometric drawing (Office of Dan Kiley, redrawn based upon 1957 plan drawing)

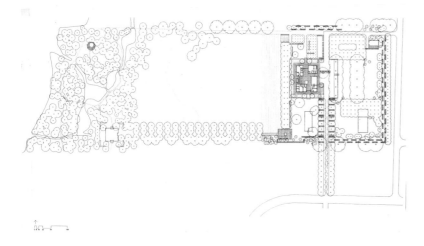

Figure 2. Miller garden, plan drawing (Gregg Bleam)

When Charles asked me to talk about Dan Kiley, he said, "Just make it personal and tell what it was like to work with Dan." My response, as those of you who know Dan will understand, was that I could fill thirty minutes just telling his jokes—such as, "I never promised you a rock garden" or "When I see stress coming, I lie down flat until it passes." Seriously, I am here as a person who has known Dan in several capacities for the past eighteen years, first as an employee, then as a designer writing about the Miller garden and the Jefferson National Expansion Memorial. During my interview with Dan, regarding the Jefferson National Expansion Memorial and the National Park Service's unfortunate decision in the 1960s to change his planting plan from triple rows of tulip poplars to Rosehill ash trees, he stated,

> Most people are not excited about the dimensions of space. The different dimensions and what they do and how they affect, when you pick trees and place them so many feet on center, this is very important, whether they're ten feet, twelve feet, fifteen feet, or eighteen feet on center. Just like the windows in the Palazzo Farnese. Those things are what make it wonderful or not, the spatial proportion.[1]

Today's talk will attempt to give you an appreciation of Kiley's "dimensions of space" by focusing upon my personal observations of Dan's use of the grid—in particular, how plant selection and spacing combine to form his poetic landscapes. For to understand why Kiley's work must be preserved, it is critical to understand how plant selection and spacing define the work.

Background Dan Kiley is arguably the most important landscape architect of our time. For more than sixty years he has created residential and institutional landscapes that are known for their elegant simplicity, geometric rigor, and poetic use of plants. His impressive list of designs includes the Jefferson National Expansion Memorial in St. Louis, Missouri; the National Gallery of Art in Washington, D.C.; the J. Irwin Miller residence in Columbus, Indiana; and Rockefeller University in New York City.

Kiley was born in 1912 in Boston, Massachusetts. (He turned ninety in September 2002.) His career began when he worked in the office of landscape architect Warren Manning from 1932 to 1938. In February of 1936 he enrolled as a special student in the landscape architecture program at Harvard University, where he encountered Garrett Eckbo and James Rose. Influenced by Walter Gropius, who was teaching at Harvard at that

Figure 3. Miller garden, redbud bosque (Alan Ward)

Figure 4. Miller garden, honey locust allée (Alan Ward)

Figure 5. Hamilton-Cosco manufacturing plant, gingko allée, view to lawn (Gregg Bleam)

Figure 6. Hamilton-Cosco manufacturing plant, gingko allée, elevation view (Gregg Bleam)

time, Kiley, Eckbo, and Rose rejected the prevalent Beaux Arts education of the era in order to explore themes related to modern art and architecture. Kiley left Harvard one year later without a diploma and moved to Washington, D.C. He began working as an associate town planner for the United States Housing Authority, and through this position he met the architect Louis Kahn, with whom he proceeded to work on several Defense War Housing projects. Kahn also introduced Kiley to another architect, Eero Saarinen, who later became an important collaborator.

Kiley left the Housing Authority in 1940 and opened the Office of Dan Kiley both in Washington, D.C., and in Middleburg, Virginia. His first commission was a garden for the forty-acre Collier residence in Falls Church, Virginia, in Kiley's words "a 'modernistic' house, but not modern."[2] For four months during the garden's realization, he lived with the Colliers, personally completing the site grading and supervising the extensive plantings.

During the war years—between 1942 and 1945—Kiley and Eero Saarinen served together in the Army Corps of Engineers in the Office of Strategic Services at Fort Belvoir. During this period Kiley collaborated on his first project with Saarinen, moonlighting on a design competition for the new Parliament building in Quito, Ecuador. In 1945 Saarinen returned to Michigan to assist his father Eliel on the design of the General Motors Technical Center.

Upon Saarinen's departure Kiley took over his position as Chief of the Design Presentation Branch and was named as the architect for the Nuremberg Trials Courtroom in Germany. This assignment afforded him the opportunity to visit Europe for the first time. While overseas, he saw the gardens of Versailles, Parc du Sceaux, and other classic seventeenth-century designs by André Le Nôtre. This exposure to Le Nôtre's work—its simplicity, restraint, and use of the grid—proved important in Kiley's development and would become the basis for his synthesis of a classical vocabulary with ideas of modern space.

Following the war, Kiley moved his office to Franconia, New Hampshire, mainly because, in his words, it offered "good skiing." In 1947 he was invited to work with Eero Saarinen on an entry for the Jefferson National Expansion Memorial competition in St. Louis, Missouri, which they won. Both architect and landscape architect benefited from the widespread attention focused on their collaborative effort, even though completion of the memorial was stalled until the early 1960s. Saarinen and Kiley would prove to be ideal collaborators, due in part to Saarinen's firm belief in the design of a "total environment" where landscape and architecture are integrated.[3] This position was not held by many architects practicing during the 1940s and 1950s, many of whom typically used plants only as a foil for their buildings rather than as structural elements to connect interior and exterior space.

Kiley completed other projects on his own in the late 1940s, including a landscape plan for the David Hamilton garden in Princeton, New Jersey, in 1949. This garden featured an entrance court with the herb thyme planted in a grid pattern. Characteristic of Dan's humor, he labeled the plan a "court of thyme and space."

The Miller Garden
In 1951 Dan moved his residence and office to Wings Point on Lake Champlain, facing the Adirondack Mountains near Charlotte, Vermont. Kiley began work with Eero Saarinen two years later on what he has described as his "first essentially modern landscape design"[4] for the residence of Mr. and Mrs. J. Irwin Miller and family. Designed between 1953 and 1957, the Miller house and garden occupy a plot of land between Washington Street and the Flatrock River in Columbus, Indiana.[5]

Kiley's design for the Miller garden represents a transformation from his early work, which had been based upon nonorthogonal geometries, to the use of the grid as the primary ordering device. An obvious influence on Kiley was the work of André Le Nôtre, who used the grid to organize his gardens in the seventeenth century. By the early part of the twentieth century, however, the grid had become a symbol of all that was modern in art and architecture. Modern architecture's focus on developing forms that decentralized space and emphasized the periphery took advantage of the continuous order allowed by the grid. The exposed structural grid of Mies van der Rohe's architecture, for example, had a strong influence on both Kiley and Saarinen.

The house, designed by Eero Saarinen and Kevin Roche, sits on an ivy-covered marble plinth placed on a level, square earthen terrace approximately fifteen feet above the floodplain. Here, Kiley extended the lines of the pinwheel plan arrangement of the interior rooms to form a structure of grids that would order the surrounding gardens. By using the classical planting forms of bosques, hedges, and allées juxtaposed against flat ground planes of crushed stone or lawn, Kiley extended the diagram of the house design to the remaining site.

Kiley's design divided this site into three parts: garden, meadow, and wood. Highly ordered geometric gardens on the upper terrace surround the house and unfold as one moves through its spaces. A staggered pattern of clipped arborvitae hedges defines the boundary on three sides of this area. An allée of honey locusts planted parallel to the west face of the house provides shade and acts as a link between a sculpture by Henry Moore to the north and a terrace and stair leading to the meadow. Small groups of weep-

ing willows punctuate the space of the meadow below. A wood adjacent to the river, consisting of floodplain trees, forms the third part of Kiley's plan. From this lower vantagepoint, due to the foreshortened view, the house appears to sit above a large square lawn. Garden, meadow and wood create a dynamic composition reminiscent of a classical tripartite order.

The house is supported by sixteen white cruciform columns arranged to form a nine-square grid. These structural columns support the steel frame, articulating the distinction between column, wall, and horizontal roof, a characteristic of Mies's mature architecture. Organized on a grid module of 2.5 feet, the free interior plan allows the four individual "houses" (or rooms) to accommodate the different programmatic needs of the inhabitants. Spatially each of these rooms pinwheels around the ambiguous center of the house, providing Kiley with a model on which to base the design of the surrounding garden.

A dense allée of horse chestnut trees—a common Le Nôtre device—leads to the entrance court of the house. The density of the horse chestnuts creates a dark tunnel of space focused upon the sunlit entrance court beyond. Bosques, clipped hedges, tapis vert, and crushed stone walks also recall the gardens of Le Nôtre. Kiley dismisses complicated explanations: "The house was designed in functional blocks, such as the kitchen, the dining room, the master bedroom, and the living room. So I took this same geometry and made rooms outside using trees in groves and allées."[6]

Kiley used a ten-foot grid to regulate the location of most of the trees and hedges, although the podium grid of the house and the regulating grid of the garden are not aligned in plan. Bosques of multitrunked redbud trees fell on this grid to form an L-shaped space defining two sides of the tapis vert in the adult garden. Other grids were used throughout the garden, many inconsistent with one another. This emphasized the independence of rooms within the garden while maintaining the spatial connections. In plan, these grids created a pattern that reinforced the centrifugal movement of space around the house. By defining a structure (the column of trees) that could be countered with walls (hedges), Kiley approximated the architectural concept of the free plan.

At the Miller garden, the grid was ideal for extending the boundaries of the building in all directions. Through its repetition, it abolished the center and moved the viewer's eyes to the periphery, implying a continuous nonhierarchical order. This functional simplicity combined with a minimal plant palette effectively guides the viewer to focus on the form and space of the garden instead of on the individual plant.

In my opinion, Kiley's most brilliant formal design idea is his unconventional use of the allée of delicately branched honey locusts planted in a twelve-by-eighteen-foot grid pattern, set parallel to the west façade of the house. Placed counter to the movement of the garden, the allée creates a transparent wall on the garden's western edge that he refers to as a "balustrade."[7] Here the grid works in two ways: first, to structure the axis between the Henry Moore sculpture and the terrace on the south; and second, to define the edge of the platform of the house.

Kiley used this formal device again in his 1964 design for the Hamilton-Cosco manufacturing plant, also located in Columbus. At Cosco, the power of the geometry of spacing plants on the grid is clear. Sentry gingko trees planted on an eighteen-by-twenty-four-foot grid define the entrance to the building while also forming a screen between the parking lot and the front lawn. The aligned tree trunks create the appearance of walls in the perspective view, then frame the surrounding landscape as one moves through the space. The allée leads one to the front door, thereby creating an elegant entrance solution.

Kiley's simple use of the allée to simultaneously define a space in at least two ways represents a brilliant synthesis of modern spatial ideas and classical structure. Speaking of this fusion, Kiley has said, "I find direct and simple expressions of function and site to be the most potent. In many cases, though not all, this has led me to design using classic geometries to order spaces that are related in a continuous spatial system that indicates connections beyond itself, ultimately with the universe."[8] His statement alludes to the relationship of the Miller garden to the gridded framework of the midwestern landscape.

Although the Miller garden is meticulously maintained, several changes have compromised Kiley's intentions for the adult garden. The Japanese holly hedges, which had originally been situated in the adult garden within the square grid of redbud tree trunks, were removed. Unfortunately, upon the removal of Kiley's "pinwheel" hedges from the adult garden and the replacement of the grove of multitrunked redbuds with single-stemmed crabapples, the ideas of spatial continuum and free-plan space were lost in this portion of the garden. Kiley has stated that "the major thing that changed was on the west side looking across toward the sculpture and the redbud grove. I had Mies van der Rohe-like hedges there before they were removed. This did a lot to spatially define the lawn and define the space."[9]

Even before the completion of the Miller garden in 1957, Kiley would have the opportunity to continue these explorations with the acceptance of his first commission in New York City, to complete a master plan for Rockefeller University.

Rockefeller University Founded in 1901 by John D. Rockefeller, Rockefeller University is located on the east side of Manhattan on York Avenue. In 1906 Shepley Rutan and Coolidge completed Founders Hall, located on the main entrance road from Sixty-sixth Street. Buildings were sited at the highest elevation of the property, taking advantage of the flat terrain and capitalizing on views of the East River. In 1910 the main entrance allée of London plane trees and the single cross-axis row of trees were planted. These trees would later prove critical to Kiley's plan.

Kiley began working on the project in 1956, along with the architect Wallace K. Harrison and Detlev Bronk. Their task was to site three new buildings, develop the master plan, and create planting schemes for the fourteen-acre site. Bronk, then a member of the Rockefeller Board of Scientific Directors, said at the time, "I have always felt that science should be recognized for the beauty of its spiritual undertaking. I believe that science benefits from being carried on in a lovely setting."[10] At Rockefeller University, Kiley chose the Beaux Arts geometry of the original campus plan as an organizational device, siting Abby Aldrich Rockefeller Hall, Caspary Hall, and the Graduate Student Residence adjacent to the magnificent row of previously planted London plane trees. Kiley created a flat expanse of lawn at the core of the campus, bordered by a marble walk.

Sectionally, the campus was developed on two levels. On the upper level small courtyards and gardens connected to the central academic promenade, which was organized along the existing row of plane trees ending in an esplanade and "floating stair." At this level, Kiley used the existing row of trees to form a "wall" or vertical plane while creating a rhythm in the repetition of the individual trunks on close centers. Below the Graduate Student Housing Kiley extended the geometry of the building grid to lay out an allée of plane trees on a ten-by-twelve-foot grid, which, due to their open-branching canopy, created a wonderful pattern of shadows along the walk.

The lower (street) level contains what is perhaps Dan's most important work in New York City, the Philosopher's Garden. Adjacent to New York Avenue, this sunken garden reminds one of the Asian walled garden Kiley has described as an urban oasis:[11] Double rows of European hornbeams line a marble terrace; nearby, flat pool surfaces punctuated by vertical water jets create a soothing sense of calm seclusion.

Lincoln Center After completing the design for Rockefeller University, Kiley joined the design team for Lincoln Center in 1960. He was first brought into the project to work with Eero Saarinen on the North Court in front of the Beaumont Theater. As the project progressed, Kiley's role grew to include the landscape of Lincoln Center as a whole. Ken Smith has documented the decline of this landscape in

Figure 7. Rockefeller University, London plane trees at main entrance (Office of Dan Kiley)

Figure 8. Rockefeller University, London plane tree allée adjacent to Graduate Student Housing (Gregg Bleam)

Figure 9. Lincoln Center, Bradford pear tree planting, 2002 (Gregg Bleam)

his essay, "The Challenge of Preserving Lincoln Center for the Performing Arts."[12]

The North Court relates directly to Saarinen's theater. An 80-by-120-foot pool mirrors the Henry Moore as it emerges from the water and is framed by an L-shaped plan of twenty-foot-square travertine-clad planting boxes that double as seat walls and provide additional soil depth over the parking lot below. Originally, a quartet planting of London plane trees was spaced at twelve feet on center in each planter box, the tree spacing integrating the surrounding architectural order. Red and white azaleas were planted below the trees to unify the raised ground plane. A third line of quartets lined the court's north side at the top of the wall and steps leading to the Julliard School Bridge.

In his monograph Kiley says, "Eventually, the plane trees were replaced with a single Bradford pear tree in each four-hundred-square-foot box. Sadly, this action emasculated the volumetric power of the original planting plan and severed the link between the architecture of

Figure 10. Lincoln Center, Kiley's original quartet plantings of London plane trees (Office of Dan Kiley)

76

Figure 11. Office of Dan Kiley, March 1986 (Gregg Bleam)

plantings and buildings that together form a civic space of integrity."[13] Damrosch Park, although not detailed by Kiley's office, was also a part of Kiley's original concept for Lincoln Center. The bandstand and the Big Apple Circus have placed additional stress on the remaining quartet plantings. Despite the obvious need for events such as these to occur in the city, they have compromised the integrity of the space as a whole.

Given the importance of planting spacing to achieve spatial intent, Lincoln Center raises critical preservation issues related to Kiley projects for the planting geometry was compromised in the interest of providing more planting soil for each tree and reducing tree-pruning maintenance, a very pragmatic approach from a horticultural and budgetary point of view. However, the Kiley landscape has been greatly diminished, if not completely lost. The larger question for institutions with aging Kiley landscapes will be whether there is a financial commitment to preserve the design intent. Institutions operating on

limited landscape budgets might be tempted to space replacement trees farther apart in the interest of reducing costs, but doing so will destroy dynamic spatial qualities that only occur with Kiley's closely-spaced planting-plan geometries.

Office of Dan Kiley 1985–1987 I will never forget the first words that I heard Dan Kiley speak, in the spring of 1984, when Michael Van Valkenburgh, my professor of landscape architecture at the Harvard Design School, invited him to say a few words to our studio: "Half of you should leave this room because you don't have what it takes to become a landscape architect." At that time Van Valkenburgh and photographer Alan Ward were preparing for the opening of their exhibit, "Built Landscapes: Gardens of the Northeast," which featured Kiley's Miller garden and Currier farm. I came to know Kiley's work through the all-white models and crisply drawn ink plans of the exhibit. I was impressed by the elegant simplicity of both of these projects and was fascinated

Figure 12. Parc du Sceaux, France (Gregg Bleam)

with Kiley's mastery of the grid as an organizational device and his thoughtful selection of plants. I also remember being somewhat taken aback by Kiley's departure from convention, with his long white hair, his slightly rumpled attire, and his outrageous views. He made statements such as "The profession of landscape architecture ought to be abolished" and "The best landscape architects are architects," and he even threatened to bring bodily harm to the garden designer Capability Brown, were he still alive.

A year after graduation from the Harvard Design School I was working at Sasaki Associates in Watertown, Massachusetts, when I heard that Dan Kiley might have an opening. I spoke with my classmate Peter Schaudt, and he urged me to apply for the position. So, on a beautiful June day, my wife and I made the four-hour trek from Boston to Charlotte, Vermont. I am not sure what I thought Dan's office would be like (maybe a minimalist white box), but I was taken aback by the rural if not rustic qualities of Dan's office and house. In the end Dan hired me and I began my two years in Charlotte, Vermont, by working on the Joslyn Art Museum in Omaha, Nebraska.

Later I worked on the National Sculpture Garden (unbuilt). I remember riding in the backseat of a car with Dan enroute to Collegeville, Minnesota, for a meeting at St. John's University, when Dan noted me flipping through my sketchbook. He pulled the book away from me, scanned my drawings, closed the book, and said, "Get the diagram right first," a phrase that I have never forgotten.

In the course of working on St. John's University we were faced with a campus that had several Marcel Breuer buildings. Although the buildings had a gridded, orthogonal orientation, the planting structure was absent. Dan's approach was to create hierarchy through new plantings of primarily native trees planted in allées and bosques, with arborvitae hedges creating "gardens of cars." I remember being very moved by the juxtaposition of the gridded landscape against the wildness of the northern pine woodlands. While we were working on St. John's, Dan received an announcement about an A.E. Bye lecture. He came down from his office to the studio upon reading it, and pointing to the wooded native landscape in our immediate view, he forcefully remarked, "How could anyone be so arrogant as to try to make that! I could never do that, so I don't even try. Instead, I use geometry." In working with Dan on St. John's, the grid was the organizing element, as with the majority of the projects we were working on. We knew the vocabulary to use—allée, bosque, hedge, and tapis vert. We often worked in model and hoped that we would be able to finish the model and send it out before Dan changed his mind.

Also during my time in Dan's office, I worked on the NCNB Bank project with Harry Wolf. We built models of the tartan-gridded ground plane based upon the golden section and the Fibonacci number system. The ground-plane pattern was the building façade laid flat on the ground, thereby uniting the geometry of the vertical and horizontal dimensions of the site. Dan proposed a channel of water with smaller water rills that would extend into the flat expanse of lawn. Allées of palm trees flank each walk as heroic columns, while groves of white-flowering crape myrtles organize a series of spaces within the plaza. I remember our debate within the office about placing these trees "off the grid." Dan originally had them creating a grid pattern, but later (with urging by the staff) changed them to a random pattern. This off-grid placement of trees created smaller rooms of dappled light within the groves and kept the space from becoming static.

In closing, the experience of working with Dan Kiley is one that I will always treasure. Working with Dan reinforced my own interest in geometry and the "dimensions of space," giving me a greater understanding of the power of simplicity. Since leaving Dan's office and beginning my own practice in Charlottesville, Virginia, ten years ago, I have continued to see that the most important part of design is to "get the diagram right" and then to keep the power of that diagram intact. Much of Dan's work that I have shown you today can be seen as "built diagrams," and that is what makes them memorable. His gridded plantings and minimalist use of plants are not static, as some have accused, but instead, guide the viewer into an experience of the dynamic space of the landscape. I believe Dan's vision is best summarized by his observations on Le Nôtre's Parc du Sceaux, so I will leave you with his words: "The great beauty of it was the fact that it was so simple. Just a canal of water, double rows of Lombardy poplars, that's all. That's saying everything, that you don't need to do a lot of tricks to get a thing that can be enduring and strong and exalting."[14]

Gregg Bleam is a principal of Gregg Bleam Landscape Architects, Charlottesville, Virginia, and currently a visiting critic at the University of Virginia School of Architecture.

NOTES

1 Dan Kiley, interview with the author, 2 June 1990.

2 Dan Kiley, interview with the author, 1 June 1990.

3 Aline Saarinen, ed., *Eero Saarinen on His Work* (New Haven: Yale University Press, 1968), p. 6.

4 Dan Kiley, "Miller Garden," *Process Architecture*, 1982, 21.

5 For a more extensive design analysis of the Miller garden, see Gregg Bleam, "Modern and Classical Themes in the Work of Dan Kiley" in Marc Treib, ed., *Modern Landscape Architecture: A Critical Review* (Cambridge: The MIT Press, 1993), pp. 220-39.

6 Dan Kiley in Warren T. Byrd and Reuben Rainey, eds., *The Works of Dan Kiley: A Dialogue on Design Theory* (Charlottesville: The University of Virginia, School of Architecture, 1983), p. 14.

7 See Byrd and Rainey, eds., *The Works of Dan Kiley*, p. 30.

8 Dan Kiley, "My Design Process," *Process Architecture*, 15.

9 Dan Kiley, interview with the author, 2 June 1990.

10 Rockefeller University, Master Plan 2000, draft, p. 10.

11 Dan Kiley and Jane Amidon, *Dan Kiley: The Complete Works of America's Master Landscape Architect* (New York: Little, Brown and Company, 1999), p. 33.

12 Ken Smith, "The Challenge of Preserving Lincoln Center for the Performing Arts," *Preserving Modern Landscape Architecture* (Cambridge: Spacemaker Press, 1999), pp. 50-52.

13 See Kiley, *Dan Kiley: The Complete Works of America's Master Landscape Architect*, p. 57.

14 Dan Kiley, interview with the author, 2 June 1990. Author's Note: Although Kiley cites the beauty of the Lombardy poplar plantings at Parc du Sceaux, recent research has revealed that the Lombardy poplars were not planted by Le Nôtre but in the 1900s, after Le Nôtre's death. See Marc Treib, "The Care and Feeding of the NobleAllée", in *Arnoldia*, 54, 1, 1994, 12–18.

New Parks for New York

Donald Richardson

Figure 1. *Sculpture Garden, Modern Museum of Art, New York City (Zion Breen & Richardson Associates)*

The firm of Zion Breen & Richardson has been in business for forty-six years and has completed numerous projects. It would be impossible to cover those forty-six years in thirty-five minutes so I will try to give an overview of the firm's general design philosophy and examine the steps taken by the firm in the development of three urban landscape architectural projects located in midtown New York City: Paley Park, the IBM Building Atrium, and the Museum of Modern Art Sculpture Garden. I will identify the driving forces behind the design of each project, the reasons these projects have endured for many years, and the teamwork it took to complete them.

The firm of Zion & Breen was founded in New York City in 1957 by Robert Zion, who had worked with I. M. Pei. He recruited Harold Breen as a partner. Together they embarked on numerous projects throughout the New York region. I joined the firm in 1961, after seeing the firm's work at Roosevelt Field Shopping Center on Long Island on a class trip from the Harvard Design School. The simplicity and quality of the design impressed me. Harold Breen died in 1996, and Robert Zion continued to manage the firm. After his death in 2000, the business continued under my leadership, operating under the name of Zion Breen & Richardson Associates.

I would like to share with the group the story of how Robert Zion became involved in the profession of landscape architecture. Bob was in college during World War II and was drafted into the army. He was assigned to Washington, D.C., as a translator of Chinese. He was later reassigned to Europe during the Battle of the Bulge. He suffered from diarrhea throughout his tour in Europe; therefore, no one would stay in the foxhole with him. One night, when he was all alone, he heard movement in the dark. He opened fire and continued shooting throughout the night. The next morning, he discovered he had shot down all the trees in the hedgerow in front of him. He was thankful to be alive and thankful that he had survived the night. He decided to become a landscape architect to restore the landscape he destroyed that night. Bob returned to Harvard and received five degrees on the G.I. Bill. One was a master's degree in landscape architecture.

As a result of his English degree from Harvard, Bob was a prolific writer. He published numerous articles about the improvement of our cities. One entitled "Some Impractical Ideas for the Improvement of Cities," published in the *AIA Journal* in February 1962, put forward the need to build parklets and zoolets and called for recognition of New York's waterfront. As Paul Friedberg noted, Bob was in the forefront in articulating the need for new urban parks on a smaller scale than Central Park, located closer to where people worked and lived.

Figure 2. Paley Park, New York City (Zion Breen & Richardson Associates)

We are often able to blot from consciousness the inconvenience, lack of amenity, and even ugliness that confront us as we go about our daily work. Most of us "get used to" these unattractive aspects of our environment. This is fortunate indeed, for without this ability many of us would find it difficult or impossible to survive. This fortunate human faculty, however, has one serious drawback: Once we "get used to" conditions as they are, we can never again see our houses, schools, or cities as others see them. The impetus to improve slowly fades. It then takes an outsider to show us how our friends, our guests, our clients perceive our environment. To this end, we analyze every project, illustrating its good as well as its bad aspects. Such an analysis is intended to refresh the awareness of those who live or work on a property but who now tend to overlook its failings—and its beauty.

In designing or redesigning any project, it is the task of the landscape architect to place himself in the role of all those who will use or view the property. This role-playing is, in our opinion, essential to good design. For a residential client, the landscape architect must, in his mind, become a friend, a child, a guest; for a school, he must be a student, a professor, a parent; for a commercial property, he must be a client, an employee. Only if a landscape is then designed to the needs and desires of those who will use it can it succeed.

The design should be fresh and not overdesigned, serenely simple yet dynamic. It should create a clear functional statement for the people participating in the design. Basically we are creating an "outdoor room" made up of floor, walls, and ceiling, and of course the furniture to serve the needs of the participants. It should capture and entertain all of the user's senses in its design, including taste, touch, smell, audio, and, of course, visual. Equally important in influencing design are people: how they behave, walk, and observe, how they can be restrained and guided.

Lastly, recognize the need. How do office workers in midtown New York spend their lunch hour? Where can they find outdoor relaxation chatting in the shade of a tree? Where in our commercial districts can a tired shopper pause for a moment's rest?

Paley Park, 1967 In 1963 the firm proposed the concept of a network of small midtown parks (vest-pocket parks) in an exhibition presented at the Architectural League of New York, sponsored by the League and the Park Association of New York. The firm was looking for vacant parcels of land (parking lots) in New York to build a prototype park. William S. Paley, president of CBS, visited the exhibit and called to inform us that he had a site for a vest-pocket park: the old Stork Club building, which was still standing on East Fifty-third Street. Paley's father had recently

Figure 3. Bamboo Garden, IBM Atrium, New York City (Peter Mauss/Esto)

died. Bob Zion talked with Paley about making the park as a memorial for his father, making an open space for the people of New York instead of erecting another statue in Central Park.

The park size is 50 feet by 100 feet (one tenth of an acre) constructed at a cost of $750,000 in 1967. The location is Fifty-third Street just east of Fifth Avenue and the Museum of Modern Art. The purpose of the park is for people, for rest, and enjoyment. The park was designed as a simple "outdoor room." The floor was granite block with sand joints until Babe Paley's high heels caught in the joints. Then that pavement was replaced with granite durax block with mortared joints and a smooth granite border. The purpose of the sand joints was to allow water to flow to the trees' root systems. After the joints were sealed, watering devices had to be installed. The walls are covered with vines (English ivy) to create a "vertical lawn." The ceiling is a dense canopy of leaves provided by the locust trees planted twelve to fifteen feet apart. The furniture did not include traditional park benches, but, rather, single chairs and tables, light and portable, as in Parisian parks. Kiosks are located at the entrance for drinks and food, important for encouraging people to linger with a cup of coffee and a hot dog (the brand personally selected by Mr. Paley). Located on the rear wall, the twenty-foot-high water wall is the most distinctive element in the park. Water tumbles over stone creating a roaring cascade, not only delightful in itself but also effective in drowning out the harsh sounds of traffic and other unpleasant city noises. Three thousand five hundred gallons of water are recirculated over the wall every minute.

William H. Whyte completed a time-lapse photo analysis of the people using the park after it was completed and found that it was the most heavily used open space, on a per-square-foot basis, in all of New York due to its location and design.

The maintenance and perpetual care of the park was arranged by the William S. Paley Foundation in memory of Mr. Paley's father. Several other vest-pocket parks have since been built near Paley Park. The small-park concept can be an important amenity only if repeated frequently. For such parks to contribute effectively to life in the city, they must be in close proximity to the users as well as profuse in number.

IBM World Headquarters Atrium, 1983
A bamboo garden in a large ground-level atrium provides office workers and the public a serene, restful oasis in busy Midtown Manhattan. The architect, Edward Larrabee Barnes, designed this corporate plaza, and Zion Breen & Richardson collaborated to create a garden that contains eleven bamboo groves rising from cutouts in the plaza pavement. The planting was intended to create a contrast to the harshness of the surrounding architecture and allow intimate seating areas for the public. The same design principles outlined in Paley Park were incorporated in the design of the bamboo garden. IBM sold the building in the 1990s, and the new owners removed a few of the bamboo groves and introduced sculpture; the garden, however, remains essentially as designed.

Museum of Modern Art, 1961 to present
Zion Breen & Richardson has been a consultant to the museum on an annual retainer since the early 1960s. The firm consulted with Philip Johnson for the additions to the museum garden in 1965 and with Cesar Pelli, architect for the Museum Tower addition, in 1982. The firm directed the 1989 renovation of the garden for the museum's fiftieth anniversary celebration.

The museum is presently involved in an extensive renovation and expansion of the building scheduled to be completed in 2004. The Sculpture Garden was removed to allow for a temporary construction staging area for this project and for the introduction of new underground utilities, rooms, duct banks, etcetera. The firm of Zion Breen & Richardson Associates is currently consulting with the museum and architects to re-create the garden. The existing trees were transplanted from the garden to the New York Botanical Garden as a gift from the museum. Yoshio Taniguchi, the architect, was awarded the contract in a recent competition for the design of the new additions in collaboration with Kohn Pedersen Fox Associates. The Sculpture Garden is approximately 100 feet by 250 feet on three levels. After numerous meetings with the museum staff and architects, including Philip Johnson, it was decided that the garden, the main focus of the museum, would be re-created to its 1982 design, adapting to new architectural changes as required.

The garden is a multiuse outdoor space, providing a setting for the ever-changing sculpture and art exhibits, fund-raising, concert events, and a pleasant outdoor room for sitting, viewing, contemplation, and, of course, a great place to meet for lunch. The new plantings of weeping European beech, birch, and London plane trees, pavement (unpolished gray marble), reflecting pools, and fountains will be restored to their original design. Viewed from the surrounding galleries, museum restaurants, the residential tower, and the public street, the garden is a sculptural element in itself and an oasis worthy of re-creating and preserving.

The Firm Services of the firm include all aspects of site planning and landscape architecture. Completed projects of the firm include town planning, urban parks and plazas, school and university campuses, corporate headquarters, residential properties, indoor and rooftop plantings, and sculpture gardens. The firm has been honored with more than fifty national and regional awards for design excellence.

The Mill In 1973 Salter's Mill, a 300-year-old structure in Imlaystown, New Jersey, was slated for demolition. Bob Zion purchased the landmark and restored it. The office moved from New York City to the Mill. Zion had purchased a nearby farm and was determined to realize his dream of commuting to work on horseback. This historic building with the millrace coursing below us, views of a lake, and the surrounding rural countryside provides a work environment favorable to our approach to design.

Donald Richardson, FASLA, is a principal of Zion Breen & Richardson Associates, landscape architects and site planners in Imlaystown, New Jersey. He is a graduate of Delaware Valley College and the Harvard Design School.

The Nature of Modernity: Principles for Keeping Historic Landscapes Alive

Grant R. Jones

Understanding the nature of modernity necessitates many questions. Why should we preserve the landscape architectural remains of the modern movement? This republic began in the wilderness by throwing out European history, long before Europeans themselves revolted against the pretense of their historic culture. Before World War II, Bauhaus architects had been deeply influenced by Frank Lloyd Wright. America's innovative genius had already undermined Europe's historical fantasies.

Does modernism make a break with nature? To explore this question requires perspective on American tradition. We did not see our progress toward the American Dream as an act of destruction. Likewise we do not now see these built works as necessarily worth preserving for their own sake. Our Founding Fathers knew they were a revolutionary generation and have often been quoted as saying the end of history is now at hand. Should modern landscapes survive when they are no longer modern? Works of architecture stand apart from their settings as objects of their cultural periods. When the setting evolves with ongoing culture, the architectural object survives and is often protected as an artifact of its period, often because it can be recycled to serve contemporary tenants.

How can works of landscape architecture be preserved? They have a broader mission, usually, less separable from their setting. In fact, landscape architectural works often make a contract with nature. The ethics of landscape architecture expand beyond the missions of historic preservation. And so I want to ask a fourth question.

Is landscape architecture too fertile for modernism? There are those who say that modernism makes a break with nature by tailoring a setting for human use, by celebrating human industry, not nature, and it can be preserved like any work of art. However, the ethics of preservation keep evolving. The National Park Service experts have difficulty keeping up. They are criticized on the one hand for their wasteful attempts to maintain an object frozen in time and on the other for their benign neglect of priceless resources.

Art Nouveau was launched in the 1890s, a wedding of the clean, unbroken lines of the machine with a linear aesthetic derived from Nature—a conscious response to the need for an art that was truly modern. Modernism, its offspring, has a more than implied reciprocity with nature. Lewis Mumford's writings on the modern house as a biological institution were presented at the International Exhibition at the Museum of Modern Art, New York City, in the spring of 1932. He established the modern house as a shelter for reproduction, nutrition, and recreation. Along with gardens and playground, it could translate essential biological requirements into concrete equivalents, such as direct exposure to sunlight, air, and views from the living room to the garden.

Figure 1. Pioneer Square Park, Seattle, Washington, circa 1915 (Seattle Historical Society)

Figure 2. *The Plan for Two Parks by Ilze Jones and Grant Jones of Jones & Jones, 1971 (Photographs, Jones and Jones Architects and Landscape Architects, Ltd)*

Figure 3. *Pergola restored in 1972 by Jones & Jones*

Figure 4. *Tsimshian carver Jack Hudson, from Metlakatla, restored the ancient Tlingit pole.*

Figure 5. *Site of Occidental Square Park*

Figure 6. The Seattle music scene in Occidental Park

Figure 7. The pergola's base is pruned back and the social territories edited out in 1998.

Figure 8. The Modern Vision: ink drawing by Ilze Jones of Seattle's first European cobblestone square

Figure 9. The repose at Occidental Square Park during Christmas under the maturing London plane trees, 1982

Figure 10. Restored hooped benches

Figure 11. Making contact with nature

Mumford saw modern architecture and landscape architecture as integrated, with the land and with human beings.

What is the nature of modernity? Modernity makes a break with history, but not with nature. In fact, it often sets the stage for a dance with nature, leading to a new marriage with nature that won't look like any other that preceded it. Think how Van Gogh opened our eyes. How Hans Arp and Joan Miro and Man Ray helped us see inside to the essence of nature. How Alexander Calder captured nature's elements. How Antonio Gaudi celebrated nature with religious fervor in Barcelona. How Georgia O'Keefe undressed the deserts of New Mexico. At its best, modern landscape architecture is a revolution whose champion is evolution. Evolution describes the efforts of all living things to reach out for partners, in part and as a whole, to evolve to ever-higher potential. So, in my definition, modern landscapes must be living, evolving, cultural landscapes, reaching out for partners.

How can principles of historic preservation be adapted to serve these living, evolving modern landscapes? To meet the test of nature, original works of landscape architecture should evolve. Our institutions, which support them, need to evolve as well. Freezing places in time insures their demise as settings for living culture. Benign neglect is equally terminating. Stewardship implies maintaining works of landscape architecture as living cultural landscapes, by retaining the counsel of the original designers or their disciples as well as by encouraging future designers who are willing and able to respect and play by the rules of the original work.

Long ago on Puget Sound white men founded a town and named it after an American Indian: Chief Sealth. They called their first cabin site New York Alki because they believed it would be New York City someday. Alki meant "by and by" in the chief's tongue. Their New York tongues could not pronounce Sealth; they called it Seattle. In 1914 a revolutionary triangular space was built in Seattle. In it was a large cast-iron pergola with a glass canopy that sheltered the largest comfort station west of the Mississippi. It was underground, replete with fifteen water closets for ladies, a similar number for gentlemen along with eighteen urinals plus a cigar store and shoeshine parlor. At the tip of the triangle was a totem stolen from the Tlingit tribe in British Columbia. Both the pergola and the totem pole were near collapse in 1970. James Casey, founder of United Parcel Service (UPS), which he started in Seattle in 1907, gave a grant to the City to restore Pioneer Square Park, sans the underground comfort station.

Ground rules for increasing the health, viability, and potential of pioneering works of landscape architecture need to address several questions: How can this landscape allow for contemporary objects and activities to be made at home? What can be done to encourage new generations to recip-

rocate with it? Does it make a home for us to experience the four worlds: the Natural World, the Animal World, the Human World, and the Spirit World? In other words, does it continue to make connections to nature, to reach up and bring down the sky, to connect us to the mountains, to give us the warmth of the sun, cool us with shade, capture the caress of the wind, give us reflections and the sound of falling water? Does it make a home for birds and insects and the flow of life? Does it invite us to shape our lives with others, to nourish our humanity as a place to relax and feel safe? Does it invite us to learn to respect those who came before us, to reflect, to give thanks to the Creator, to the great forces of nature that made us? What can I do not just to keep this landscape alive, but to increase the potential of the original designer's intentions? In other words, how can we adapt this living cultural landscape so that it reciprocates with nature and human society in a supportive relationship that increases nature's power and potential to sustain us humans and our living cultures for generations to come? Like the mechanisms put in place at the founding of this country, this will need to be a work in progress. As Joseph Ellis writes in his new book *Founding Brothers: The Revolutionary Generation*, "The achievement of the revolutionary generation was a collective enterprise that succeeded because of the diversity of personalities and ideologies present in the mix." So let us rise to the occasion and preserve the design spirit of our innovative works of modern landscape architecture, because as living, evolving cultural landscapes they are works in progress, reaching out for partners to sustain and increase their vitality.

Take My Hand
Beyond the open door,
Shadows bend
Whose ears hear water near that tree
Who grew a stream?
Birds appear and disappear.
My waterface makes friends
Whose eyes see clouds of wind in my hair
What is that hole?
Deepness doesn't move.
Who are those beyond the trees?
Take my hand.

Grant Jones, FASLA, landscape architect, poet, and cofounder of Jones & Jones Architects, Landscape Architects Ltd., has practiced ecological design for thirty years, pioneering in river planning, scenic-highway design, zoo design, and landscape aesthetics. He has taught and lectured at numerous universities.

Designating Modern Cultural Landscapes in Canada

Michael McClelland

In 2001 the Province of Ontario recognized a 1960s landscape designed by Sasaki, Strong and Associates as a significant landscape of cultural and heritage value. This was an important event because it appears that Sasaki's Queen's Park Complex may have been the first of his landscapes to be given protected heritage status. It was also important because Canada's legal framework for heritage protection was able to designate a relatively recent cultural landscape.

In protecting modern cultural landscapes the public sector usually plays the positive roles of educating, encouraging, and providing incentives and, in some cases, legislative controls. In Canada, the power of the public sector to play these roles is much weaker than it is in the United States. As a confederation of provinces, we have a situation in which each province has its own heritage legislation, somewhat similar to the United States. But we have no strong overriding federal heritage policies or incentives and few heritage controls on federally regulated agencies such as the postal service. Currently we have no National Register.

In the Province of Ontario the provincial government has enacted its own heritage legislation regulated by the Ministry of Culture. There is a loophole in the legislation regarding the protection of provincially-owned heritage properties. The Ministry of Culture doesn't own any property, and it cannot control the portfolios of the other ministries that do. This loophole is addressed by a protocol agreement that is modeled somewhat on the environmental-assessment process. The protocol requires consultation with the Ministry of Culture in the event of the alteration, sale, or demolition of a property. The limitations of this agreement are that it remains nonbinding and has a forty-year cut-off date, which, therefore, excludes the protection of modern cultural resources. The recognition of the Sasaki landscape demonstrates, however, that the protocol can extend beyond its limitations, if the circumstances are right.

The provincial heritage legislation delegates much of its authority for heritage preservation to the local municipalities, but it gives them only limited powers. Two significant shortcomings are that the Ontario Heritage Act lacks permanent demolition control and almost entirely ignores the conservation of landscapes.

While this may all sound terribly negative, it is interesting to consider the Sasaki designation and to note that Canada has a fairly good track record in heritage preservation. It may be precisely because of this soft legislative framework that there is a willingness to cooperate and to find an accepted ground for negotiation.

Cities like Toronto have used their provincial heritage legislation as broadly as possible. Toronto City Council frequently designates recent

Figure 1. Queen's Park Complex, Toronto, Canada, construction aerial, 1970s, showing the northeast corner of the site: The three smaller blocks with the taller tower form the Queen's Park Complex. (Provincial Archives of Ontario & Ontario Realty Corp.)

Figure 2. Conceptual sketch of the site from southwest showing the Whitney Block to the left (Provincial Archives of Ontario & Ontario Realty Corp.)

Figure 3. Conceptual sketch from the southwest showing the original plaza design, which was not executed (Provincial Archives of Ontario & Ontario Realty Corp.)

properties. Its current move to designate Mies van der Rohe's TD Centre is regarded as an anomaly because most Torotonians assume that it must have done so years ago. The Council designated the 1964 New City Hall and its plaza, called Nathan Phillips Square, as a heritage property in the mid-1970s, about ten years after construction and as soon as the provincial act came into force. It states simply that municipalities can protect properties of "architectural and historical value or interest," and the City of Toronto decided that architectural value could potentially rest with significant designs, landscape or building, new or old, without regard to any stated age limit. Municipalities like Toronto have frequently designated provincially-owned properties, like the Queen's Park Complex, even though they are aware municipalities can have no legal power over the actions of the province.

The roles of the different levels of government can be seen at work in the evaluation of Sasaki's landscape at the Queen's Park Complex. It is a provincially-owned property built not quite forty years ago, started in the early 1960s and completed in 1971. The federal government plays no role, even though the property might arguably have some potential for national significance. The provincial agency that owns the property, the Ontario Realty Corporation, plays a guarded role, encouraged and cajoled by the Ministry of Culture. The local municipality plays the role of advocate-observer.

The Queen's Park Complex was built as the second annex building to the Provincial Legislature located in downtown Toronto. The Provincial Legislature itself is a large Richardsonian Romanesque building and its grounds are called Queen's Park. In the early 1990s, the Office of the Speaker of the House developed, without any prompting, its own heritage master plan for the Provincial Legislature and its grounds. The Speaker did this as a direct attempt to ensure appropriate preservation measures for a significant provincially-owned property. It may also have been intended as a demonstration of responsible public stewardship, acknowledging the lack of any legal obligation toward preservation.

Directly to the east of Queen's Park is the first annex building, the Whitney Block, built in the 1920s. When it was slated for substantial alterations in the mid-1990s the Ministry of Culture requested the provincial protocol be undertaken, argued partly on the basis of the building's proximity to the Provincial Legislature. The protocol was followed, and a heritage master plan was adopted for the Whitney Block.

It later became clear, however, that the Whitney Block's heritage master plan was not catching all of the changes to the landscape in its vicinity. After the erection of a very large police memorial and proposed ad hoc landscape improvements to deal with skateboarders, vandalism,

Figure 4. Current planting at the northeast corner of the site, before restoration (ENVision—The Hough Group)

Figure 5. View of landscaping in the northeast corner of the site (ENVision—The Hough Group)

Figure 6. Whitney Block Court, xeriscaped modifications in the southwest corner of the site (Provincial Archives of Ontario & Ontario Realty Corp.)

Figure 7. View of the enclosed interior courtyard (ENVision—The Hough Group)

Figure 8. Water feature in the northeast court (ENVision—The Hough Group)

Figure 9. One of the public art pieces, "The Three Graces," bronze sculpture by Gerald Gladstone (ENVision—The Hough Group)

Figure 10. *Early view of the enclosed courtyard, 1970s (Provincial Archives of Ontario & Ontario Realty Corp.)*

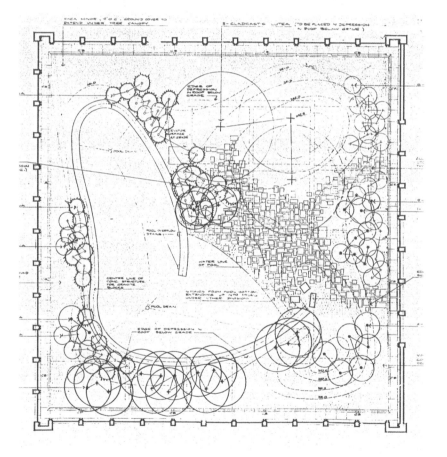

Figure 11. *Sasaki plan for the interior courtyard (Provincial Archives of Ontario & Ontario Realty Corp.)*

and tripping hazards, the Ministry of Culture again requested that the protocol be followed. This time the evaluation would look at the heritage value of the landscape surrounding the Queen's Park Complex and abutting the Whitney Block. While the Queen's Park Complex was not old enough to fall technically within the guidelines for the protocol agreement, its proximity to the Provincial Legislature and its shared open space with the Whitney Block were sufficient to require the review.

The team of ERA Architects; Hough Woodland Naylor Dance Leinster, landscape architects; and Mark Laird, landscape historian, was asked to prepare the heritage landscape assessment before any of the repair work would occur. The assessment, to be submitted to the Ministry of Culture, would fulfill the protocol requirements. If it was determined that there was a cultural resource to be protected, the assessment would also include a recommended heritage master plan to be followed by the landlord agency. That plan would be implemented under the direction of the consultant team. The assessment did conclude that the landscape was a significant cultural resource, and the landlord agency, recognizing the importance of the design and the designers, agreed to the recommended master plan.

In order to follow the protocol, an advisory group was required, and the Ministry of Culture selected Docomomo Ontario, the Architectural Conservancy of Ontario, the provincial Association of Landscape Architects, and staff from the City of Toronto's Culture Division. The advisory group, along with the Ministry of Culture staff, was instrumental in supporting the recommendations and was keenly aware of the value of promoting the conservation of a modern landscape.

The Queen's Park Complex is a single building consisting of a low square podium with a central courtyard and four towers. Each of the towers extends slightly beyond the podium like the spokes of a pinwheel. Separate and distinct landscapes are found on all sides of the building as well as in the interior courtyard.

The tacit limit of the study was that it should consider only the landscape despite the fact that there is a very clear and intact design integration of building and landscape. There was considerable concern that we might pay too much attention to the Queen's Park Complex as a building and as a potential heritage structure. Interestingly, the acceptance of the landscape as heritage seemed more palatable than the still very undervalued architecture. In order to insure that the nonbinding protocol recommendations were implemented, this limit on the assessment wasn't challenged.

The Queen's Park Complex building was designed by a consortium of four of the largest Canadian architectural firms, and the complex was one

Figure 12. Conceptual sketch for the courtyard (Provincial Archives of Ontario & Ontario Realty Corp.)

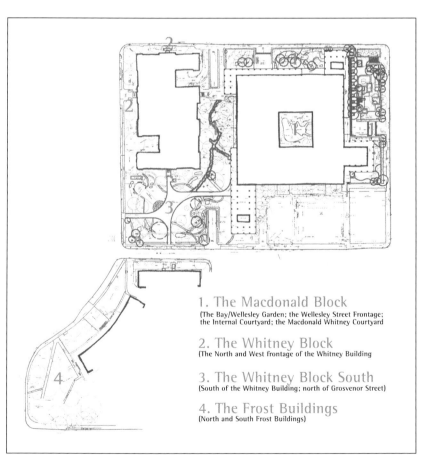

1. The Macdonald Block
(The Bay/Wellesley Garden; the Wellesley Street Frontage; the Internal Courtyard; the Macdonald Whitney Courtyard)

2. The Whitney Block
(The North and West frontage of the Whitney Building

3. The Whitney Block South
(South of the Whitney Building; north of Grosvenor Street)

4. The Frost Buildings
(North and South Frost Buildings)

Figure 13. Site plan showing the podium plan, Queen's Park Complex, labeled The MacDonald Block, with the Whitney to the left (Provincial Archives of Ontario & Ontario Realty Corp.)

of the province's largest architectural projects during the 1960s. The landscape was developed as a master plan by Sasaki, Strong and Associates, with Hideo Sasaki credited as the designer. Sasaki, Strong and Associates was a Toronto branch office of the Sasaki organization. The branch was formed in 1962 in partnership with Richard Strong as the local Canadian associate. The association continued for about five years during the major work on the complex. Richard Strong Associates completed the final phases of the project. Strong was a prominent landscape architect in his own right as the founder and first chairman of the University of Toronto's Department of Landscape Architecture. His project manager, Gerry Englar, stayed with the project from 1964 until 1971, when the last work was completed. Both Strong and Englar played major roles in the development of the landscape profession in Canada.

The assessment considered both the landscape and its urban context. The Queen's Park Complex landscape is at the eastern end of a large series of interlinked and informal open spaces that meander through the city and include the University of Toronto lands and Queen's Park. This extended network is possibly the most important grouping of open spaces within the downtown core of the city.

At the larger scale the Sasaki design gave the landscape significant historical value overall. At a detailed level there were recommendations for appropriate protection for each of the individual garden areas. The northeast corner of the site was found to be one of the most intact areas, a very heavily used courtyard at a very busy intersection. Its design was carefully integrated and balanced with the architecture. There was extensive use of commissioned public art. The central fountain piece was illuminated colorfully at night and operated during the winter months to create an ice sculpture. Public art was a major component of the landscape throughout the complex, giving the province its first major collection of outdoor art.

The design of the northeast corner was credited to Hideo Sasaki with technical design by Masao Kinoshita. The heritage study's recommendation was that the court should be fully restored to its original appearance. This work has now commenced. The hard landscape, built on raised pedestals, has deteriorated and is uneven. The soft landscape, particularly the birches, requires renewal.

The landscape on the north side of the building provides a narrow band of trees with surface limestone paving leading to a main entry of one of the towers. Again, full restoration has been recommended. With the exception of the northeast court, the quite naturalistic grounds of the Queen's Park Complex are mostly built on roof slabs. This naturalistic

Figure 14. Original model showing the proposed but unexecuted plazas at the southwest corner of the site and in the forecourt of the Provincial Legislature (Provincial Archives of Ontario & Ontario Realty Corp.)

quality of the grounds, with contoured mounds and large-caliper trees, demonstrates a state-of-the-art knowledge of 1960s roof-garden technology. Much of the large-scale restorative work on the site will not occur immediately, but will be timed to occur with the repair to underground roof slabs.

Between the 1920s Whitney Block and the 1960s Queen's Park Complex, the landscape was intended to provide a very soft buffer with gently meandering limestone paths and lush plantings. Unfortunately, no one anticipated the high degree of usage the area would receive. As a result, the landscape is severely degraded. It was argued that the original design should guide the rehabilitation of this area, but that there would need to be specific modifications to respond to the increase in pedestrian usage. This means recognizing desire paths, providing better lighting, and restoring some, but not all, of the dense plantings. It was agreed that the option of exactly restoring the original landscape and restricting access ran against the more important intent of free-flowing public access around the building.

The south and western end of the landscape forms a large square court directly south of the Whitney Block. Sasaki's first design in 1964 was to construct a large limestone plaza that would be twinned with an equally large limestone plaza to be constructed in front of the Provincial Legislature. This grand move, which was never executed, would have very clearly and simply illustrated the relationship between the Provincial Legislature and the annex buildings. This design was significantly changed, however, in 1967. What was constructed was a much more modest and understated design. It had an informal parklike setting with simple but elegant plantings. The change in design provoked considerable discussion in the evaluation team. In the end, it was argued, the later design, strongly influenced by Strong and Englar, may have reflected a growing understanding and response to the site and context with a greater appreciation of the value of the Provincial Legislature grounds as they were.

The understated quality of this portion of the site led to its underappreciation, and in 1992 it was modified to be a demonstration example of a xeriscape garden. The xeriscaping has never been fully functional. This was followed in 1999 by the erection of the police memorial intended to be compatible with the xeriscaping. Based on the quality and the historical significance of the modest, but potentially pivotal modernist design, unique in Ontario, it was recommended that the xeriscaping stay for the present, representing as it does a period in the evolution of the site. Eventually, with the requirement for slab repairs, the xeriscaping should be removed, the 1960s landscape restored, and the police memorial relocated.

The greatest irony of cutting off the landscape from the building in the assessment process, especially with a design in which the integration of the two is the heart of the scheme, is that the interior courtyard fell to the building side and was initially excluded from the landscape evaluation process. The interior courtyard has, in some ways, always been unavailable to the public, being a courtyard that was mostly looked into rather than entered. It was pointed out that the courtyard, poorly tended for decades, was in need of recording, restoration, and maintenance.

It is hoped that as this project proceeds there will develop a stronger understanding of the relationship of building to landscape and a greater appreciation of the collaborative nature of the Sasaki design. The process does illustrate a successful and quite Canadian form of action. It is based on advisory groups and nonbinding protocols, working with very little legislative regulation and resting almost entirely on consensus and consultation, with an understanding that there may be different objectives in play. The result is that a significant cultural resource has been recognized. There is an agreed-upon course of action to restore, maintain, and protect it.

Canada does require stronger legislative tools and stronger financial incentives to encourage preservation. For the present, our process has been effective in protecting several modern landscapes. In this case, the protocol insured that the Province of Ontario recognized the Queen's Park Complex as a significant landscape of cultural and heritage value and as the first Sasaki landscape anywhere in North America to be given protected-heritage status.

Michael McClelland is a principal of ERA Architects Inc., a Canadian architectural firm that specializes in heritage conservation and planning. He is a councilor for the Ontario Association of Architects and a course director for heritage conservation at Ryerson University in Toronto.

Figure 15. Photomontage showing the Provincial Legislature, the Whitney Block, and the towers of the Queen's Park Complex (Provincial Archives of Ontario & Ontario Realty Corp.)

Observations on a Modernist: Sir Peter Shepheard

Edward Bennis

Associating the word "modernism" with Great Britain, in fact England, produces an uncomfortable relationship. A country noted for its traditions, its conservatism, seems an unlikely bedfellow for new or radical movements; the baggage of history—particularly garden history—is not easily discarded. Yet on examination innovation has been integral to the development and the power structure of the country. Consider the Industrial Revolution and its planned industrial communities, the Garden Cities movement, interwar social housing, and the new towns of the early and mid-twentieth century; these were experimental and broke new ground in their spatial planning and architecture. But of modernism in landscape design, there are only fleeting academic and physical references. A perspective through time needs to be gained in order to understand its position.

Modernism was not at the forefront of the public or professional conscience in the aftermath of World War II; rebuilding the cities, infrastructure, and the industrial base of the nation came before experimental design ideas. David Jacques writes that the innate conservatism of the British establishment ensured that Modernist design was no more than a waking dream of the intellectual. It took the unreality of war and then reconstruction to make it seem real to the official professions of architecture and landscape architecture, certainly as far as public works and landscapes were concerned. However, when rich men and woman have chosen their own gardens, the modernism has never threatened the tradition to which Gertrude Jekyll, Percy Cane, Russell Page, and Lanning Roper belonged.[1]

Certainly modernist work in the extreme held little value for the ordinary person. Jacques referred to the prewar work of the Belgian designer Jean Caneel-Claes as asymmetric, stripped-down functionalism that looked too functional and undecorative for British tastes. The time was right and the opportunities were there for new ideas to flourish in postwar Britain. However, the years of conflict and damage produced the opposite reaction, in which the desire was to escape to the comfort and safety within the ideas of the past rather than to look forward to an unknown and unsettled future.

This lack of development during the twentieth century is apparent within English Heritage's "Register of Historic Parks and Gardens in England."[2] The register was started in 1985 and was based on the long-standing register for historic structures, although there are significant differences in terms of statutory protection.[3] Initially, the register identified the most important, and normally the most familiar to the public, of the country's historic parks and gardens. This included such sites as Stourhead, Blenheim Palace, and Fountains Abbey/Studley Royal. While

Figure1. Longwood Gardens, Kennett Square, Pennsylvania: The line between modernism and classicism is blurred in Shepheard's new entrance. (All photographs, Ed Bennis)

it was an important step forward in the recognition of landscapes as socially and artistically designed pieces, it was a predictable list, one that concentrated principally on the typology of the great house, garden, and park. Ten years later, in 1995, English Heritage held a major review and updating of the register with the specific objective of broadening the types of listed parks and gardens.[4] The approach was about the designed landscape, rather than park and garden, and was expanded to take in urban spaces, institutional landscapes, cemeteries, etcetera. In addition to broadening the range of landscape types, the appointed consultants were asked to identify modern landscapes. English Heritage operates on a thirty-year rolling dateline for listing as compared to the fifty-year date-line in the United States. In exceptional cases, and usually when sites are under direct threat, it is possible to register sites under thirty years old.[5]

In attempting to identify modern landscapes, basically those of the postwar period, it became clear that the methodology employed for identifying older landscapes was not appropriate for more recent work.

Traditional methods relied on surveys of period maps and recommendations by County Conservation Officers and special interest groups such as the Georgian Society, the Victorian Society and the Twentieth Century Society. The highly detailed maps of six inches equals one mile and twenty-five inches equals one mile, which were so useful, ceased production shortly after World War I. After this date, maps provided far less information, there was a reduction in scale of most modern work, and hence it was impossible to identify it through map evidence. In terms of individuals and groups, few conservation officers had knowledge or interest in landscapes, much less modern ones. Similarly, the societies were very much focused on their time periods and on buildings. Since contracts for the consultancy work were tight in terms of time and money, few of the more modern works found their way into the main lists much less the shortlists. There are currently twelve postwar landscapes on the register.[6]

It was the Lancashire survey that provided the first serious encounter with the work of Peter Shepheard, one of the few postwar landscape archi-

Figure 2. Longwood Gardens, The Flower Garden Walk: The whispering bench provides a visual focus and an inseparable combination of ideas shared by Shepheard and Church.

Figure 3. Bessborough Gardens, London: An aluminium ring sits in the basin that allows for the sound of falling water; the area outside the ring is still and reflects the sky.

Figure 4. Bessborough Gardens, London: The fountain sits at the end of a diagonal path that bisects the park—a feature that one never does. Yet Shepheard successfully breaks the rules.

Figure 5. Bessborough Gardens, London: Shepheard introduces the sinuous line in opposition to the geometry of the square, a playful approach of contrasts and the unexpected.

tects. He and his partner, Gabby Epstein, had produced the master plan for the new campus at the University of Lancashire. It is a rare example of a fully planned and purpose-built campus—landscape, buildings, and infrastructure—by one firm in this period of time, the 1960s. Shepheard demonstrated his position in the design approach at Lancashire. He had an intense dislike for the way the professions of architecture, planning, and landscape architecture operated independently. He said, "If I am sitting at a board and somebody says, 'What are you drawing at this minute? Is it architecture, landscape, or planning?' I wouldn't know. I'd rather design buildings with a landscape. I'd rather design a building to fit in with other buildings than on a clean slate. It's the whole setting. You can't design good buildings and let the landscape go hang, and you can't rescue bad buildings by landscape. It's all tied together."[7] Despite the clarity and uniqueness of the project, at the time it was about three years within the English Heritage thirty-year band and was not under immediate threat, so the university campus failed to make the register.

Shepheard's sense of form and space, love of nature, and strong social conscience followed from his early childhood experiences. The contrasting landscapes of the Wirral and north Wales provided both industrial landscapes and natural ones respectively, while Liverpool lay on the other side of the River Mersey. Shepheard had a keen interest in plants and the environment since his childhood days. He originally intended to study the natural sciences at university, until he met an incredibly boring biologist, whereupon he decided that his future lay in architecture. Not only was his father an architect in Liverpool, but his godfather was Sir Patrick Abercrombie. He attended the Liverpool School of Architecture, where people such as Abercrombie, Gordon Stephenson, Raymond Unwin, and Clough Williams-Ellis taught. Prior to the war in 1937, Shepheard worked for Derek Bridgewater. During the war he was with the Royal Ordnance, then afterwards with the Ministry of Town and Country Planning, developing the Greater London Plan under Abercrombie. He followed this with the appointment as deputy chief architect of Stevenage New Town until 1948, when he formed a partnership with Derek Bridgewater. There was a fledgling association with landscape during this period, which was more about the use of buildings to form outdoor space. Christopher Tunnard's prewar *Gardens in the Modern Landscape*, one of the few publications that addressed the idea of a modern movement, influenced him. Tunnard wrote of the eighteenth-century understanding of the "genius of place" combined with usefulness and aesthetics, quality materials, and meeting the needs of the client. This was a substantial turnaround from the traditional British idea of garden and landscape that was firmly vested in a horticultural tradition.

Figure 6. Goldsmith's Garden, London: A sunken garden, formerly a basement, gives shelter from city noise and provides an effective suntrap.

Figure 7. Emanuel's Court, Philadelphia: A very English garden in the center of the city

Figure 8. Charleston House, Sussex: Restoration was a new area with considerable problems; Shepheard found many of the original plant types, but it was as much about atmosphere as accuracy.

Tunnard's influence is apparent in Shepheard's first landscape proposal for an Elizabethan manor house called Somerhill in Kent. In a letter and notes that accompanied the plan he explained to Lady Goldsmith his radical proposals for such a traditional site. He described how he had provided a setting for sculptures and large stones, but "for me it excludes 'conventional' garden ornaments."[8] He proposed a set of timber and plate-glass screens, similar to Tunnard's work at Hallam in Sussex and illustrated in his book. The most controversial design piece was for an informal terrace garden that would be "completely different in character from the formal garden, and indeed from any English garden that I know." Stone, gravel, and extensive herbaceous planting in a grid system picked up on modernist form and structure, but Shepheard deviated from this with an extensive use of plants. His innate love of plants and tradition came through. Shepheard commented on his unexecuted design more than fifty years later: "I was crippled with this modernist thing . . . and you had to do ghastly grids and things. This [the garden] was not connected to the house; there's the house, there's the terrace, and the steps down. It was a sort of thing that you went out of the house, down some steps, and there was this funny garden. It's a thing that I would never dream of doing now; it was totally disconnected from the house, which is awfully sad and silly. . . . I wasn't interested in doing something in keeping with the house."[9] The experiments continued in what he referred to as his first real landscape job in 1947 for the *Daily Herald* Model Homes Exhibition. An indoor exhibition, Shepheard's design was an asymmetrically balanced composition with a raised stone-paved area laid in a grid, herbaceous planting, and a wall mural framed by a dead tree. As he said, these were not the sorts of things done in those days, but the experience was useful when "I came to do it [landscape] seriously."[10]

The "serious" opportunity arose shortly, in 1951, with the Festival of Britain, set up by the Labor government as a means of offering hope for the future in the postwar reconstruction period. Gordon Patterson says that the event "above all others in the last fifty years, encapsulated for everyone a keen desire for a better future not least in landscape terms but most of all in its fundamental reexploration of the needs for visual design in everyday life."[11] Sir Hugh Casson, the chief architect, said that the design plan "was a consciously designed townscape, in the informal English tradition."[12] Frank Clark was the chief landscape consultant, with Peter Shepheard, Maria Shephard, and Peter Youngman given specific areas to design and manage. These were a group of pioneers at a time when there was barely a landscape profession. The uniqueness was that the Festival site broke from the tradition of a public-garden typology to a new form of modern public space. Shepheard liked to compare it to the experience visitors had when visiting Venice. It was a city of beautiful buildings, yet how many people went inside them? He said that people have "been outside looking at the buildings and they have been sitting in places where it is nice to sit; this became very forceful to me." Shepheard said that at "the Festival of Britain, the landscape was more important than the buildings; the real thing was the spaces between buildings. I mean that's where people were going to be, that's where they were going to see it from, that's where they were going to sit down."[13]

Three areas fell under his control, two having their basis in the modernist movement, but with traditional aspects of the English garden. The two garden areas of the Homes and Gardens pavilion were simple, sunken rectangular forms with strong horizontal planes and vertical punctuation points. Both were softened by planting, one of which Shepheard referred to as a "sitting-room garden, with York stone paths, a grass lawn, and a herbaceous border."[14] There was a basic functionalism to the design, yet the border softened the edges and reflected garden traditions. There was ornament through the planting and a focal point that lifted the design above gardening, a composition of space and form that the public could understand and emulate. Most remembered of his work at the Festival was the Moat Garden. In contrast to the geometry of his other work, this garden was adjacent to the Tea Pavilion, an essential part of any British festival. Its references came from the writings of William Robinson and the work of Holger Blom, director of the Stockholm Parks Department. This area had the wilder, more natural feel of a streambed with pebbles and boulders, while the planting was a naturalized mix of herbaceous plants for quick impact. A mixture of betula, rhus, and salix trees on the mound gave the scene a wilder and less refined look than other areas of the Festival site. This approach showed that Shepheard had not subscribed to the pure functionalism of modernism or at least that it was tempered by nature. By this time he felt that few architects were "out-and-out functionalists" and few would admit to ever having anything to do with the movement. Landscape and garden still had a place for ornament and beauty, whereas architecture had dismissed these aspects of design. In *Modern Gardens* Shepheard writes,

The functionalists made peace with their consciences in the end by saying that beauty was itself one of the functions of architecture; but architecture has others, whereas a garden has not. Nor can the garden designer eschew ornament, for the garden is itself an ornament; and even the advocate of simplicity and restraint, both admirable qualities, cannot seek for plain surfaces and simple forms when his material is Nature's own complex and rampant vegetation.[15]

Figure 9. Cheyne Walk, London: Loose, informal planting at one end of the park provided a place for a permanent exhibition of sculptures.

Figure 10. Cheyne Walk, London: "I've done some gardens that I am very proud of, quite honestly, but that's not what I really want to do. I want to make usable space."

Modern Gardens, published in 1953, provided Shepheard with the opportunity to explore landscape and garden design on the international front. Examples were drawn from Northern Europe and the United States, principally the West Coast. Some examples from Britain were used, although these seemed almost concessionary, or at best limited. It was a rare book for the time, with the images of gardens as important as Shepheard's informative and analytical text.[16] Having read *Modern Gardens*, Ian McHarg, a young professor at the University of Pennsylvania, invited Shepheard as a visiting professor in 1958.[17] This formed a turning point for Shepheard where he found support for his interest in modern design, but always tempered with tradition. His time in Philadelphia allowed Shepheard to develop and clarify his theories on landscape. In a series of lectures given at Penn, he defined six design precepts that were essential to the well-conceived and purposeful landscape. He built his lectures around the points of scale, symbols, tradition, permanence, self-regulation (sustainability), and flexibility. The roots of these precepts could be found not only in the work of Tunnard, but also in earlier writers and designers such as Jekyll, Repton, and Robinson as well as his own father, an architect, whom he referred to as a "very Georgian sort of a man."

Two London projects in the early 1960s support Shepheard's design points. They share strong similarities in terms of context, detail, and form: urban; strong geometric forms; and sparing use of vegetation, simple grass plats, sculpture, and seating. Both provided the opportunity for shelter from the surrounding roads, for they were basement sites that had been bombed during the war and remained derelict for nearly twenty years. Shepheard played on the basement effect by placing walls around the areas and visually sinking them even farther. This provided an effective sound barrier. At Goldsmith's Gardens, the smaller of the two, Shepheard said, "I had a piece of ground there, which was five or six feet below the level of everything else; if you put a four-foot wall on the top, so people could lean against it and look down, you got a kind of eight or nine foot drop. It was lovely."[18] The sunken area had buttresses that became divisions for seating overlooking a simple square piece of grass. Narrow beds at the base of the walls were filled with rambling plants to provide a wild and unkempt look as a contrast to the strict geometry of the space and the surrounding city. Equally, Cheyne Walk responded to similar problems, but the increased scale allowed for a more comprehensive treatment. Here Shepheard could incorporate the view of the adjacent church tower, provide ramp access for buggies and the disabled, and incorporate a raised pergola seating area. There was the strong geometry of form, softened through the use of abundant climbing plants, producing a representation of a slightly wild and unkempt

nature in the city. This was taken further when Shepheard included bird boxes on the walls.

His work in Britain was heavily involved in social or government housing at this time. The fashion was for high-rise buildings, but after designing his first one, he refused to build any more. He found that these structures failed to provide the basic needs of family and community life. He managed to achieve the same density of housing using four-story buildings with pitched roofs and small open courtyards. This typology started to move into his commercial work and was particularly successful in some of his campus-planning work. While he worked on New Hall at Winchester and Bishop Otter College, Chichester, as well as Keele, Liverpool, and Oxford universities, his work for the University of Lancaster was considered to be the most coherently laid out of the new university sites. Shepheard recalled his first visit to this barren site with his partner, Gabby Epstein. "We went up there on a windy day, and it was freezing cold. Every time we opened a plan, it blew away. And we said, 'Christ, what are we going to do with these students? Where are they going to sit in the sun and all that?' Well, we decided, it's got to be cloisters. All of the buildings have got to touch the ground. We then devised this system and it had an absolutely firm principle: It had a spine down the middle where everybody walked. That led everywhere. When you came into the spaces, things were square; they were rectangular courtyards and they were all slightly different. There were two or three essentials: one was that the covered way had to be continuous, the buildings had to be three or four stories high and connecting to the next one. I thought it worked very well."[19] There was little detail to the courtyards; Shepheard relied on strategically placed specimen trees or an exposed boulder to give a sense of place and distinctiveness to the squares, while unity was achieved through simplicity and similar spatial proportions.

Similarities appear in some of Shepheard's work in the United States, most of which was carried out through the 1970s and the early 1980s. In contrast to the Lancaster campus, the University of Pennsylvania was a set of existing buildings that lacked any coherent plan or vision for the external spaces. Shepheard referred to worn-out paths and grass areas that were a sea of mud when it rained and a dust bowl when it was dry. Proposals were put forward in a planning document produced by faculty and students and led by Shepheard.[20] The greatest advantages of the site were the mature parkland trees and the volume of external space. As at Lancaster, the idea of usable space became key to the proposal, places to walk, eat, study, relax, meet, and, as Shepheard likes to say, "to snooze in the sun." He used similar approaches to the paving as he had in London: natural stone to the center of walks, bordered by brick channels and granite curbs. The local blue stone had been reduced to a two-inch thickness for "value engineering." This eventually failed and was replaced with Hastings pavers, a hexagonal asphalt unit. Shepheard had originally specified this paving unit for service/access drives only. His personal interest in art provided an opportunity for a dialogue within the landscape. Sculptures were strategically placed within the spaces that not only referenced what the place was about, but also gave identity and distinctiveness to different areas. The landscape, as urban woodland, became the unifying key to a previously disjointed group of buildings and spaces. Here the buildings were the background while the landscape became the foreground.[21]

Following on from Thomas Church, Shepheard was appointed as landscape consultant to Longwood Gardens. Bill Frederick, chair of the Gardens Committee, said that Shepheard stood above all other candidates. Frederick, himself a landscape architect, later employed Shepheard in his own garden, where he designed a delightful two-story garden pavilion. During his time at Longwood, Shepheard produced numerous improvements. These were often done in a sketchbook on site and handed directly to the workmen. He commented that there were very few proper drawings done for most of the work. There were a lot of "little things, but very important." This approach demonstrates his interest in detail, but also his ability to communicate verbally and through his drawings. He always had a sketchbook with him.

At times, a thin line separates modernism from classicism, and this is apparent in the new entrance that Shepheard designed for Longwood. The building is visually strong and defensive in a classical manner, while the landscape picks up a formal axis and breaks from this as one moves to the sides. Shepheard's love of form and geometry is apparent in the landscape and reminiscent of work done for the Festival of Britain. Planting was left to the staff of Longwood and is clearly not Shepheard's work; it is stiff and formal, lacking in the softer, wilder forms that he employed with herbaceous plants. However, he was more successful in his influence on planting in other areas. His most notable piece was the remodeling of the water-lily pools (1987). He had heard that the pipe work was to be renewed at a cost of $500,000; he found this an unbelievable cost and proposed that the entire courtyard could be redone for less money. Shepheard's proposal was simplicity itself. Indeed, at first, it is difficult to understand what he did. He removed the grass, a major maintenance problem, and combined a number of smaller pools, while keeping the main central pool that held Longwood's famous hybrid Victoria water lily.[22] This resulted in an increase of fifty-two percent of growing display area. The entire area was paved in blue stone to a specif-

Figure 11. Longwood Gardens: Shepheard reduces the number of pools from thirteen to five and increases their size and the display area.

ic pattern, and the edges to the ponds were a dark blue engineering brick that was sloped slightly upwards. This gave the edge a visual and physical contrast to the paving through color and form. The effect is a paved area that floats within the courtyard rather than a courtyard with several ponds. Shepheard convinced Longwood to extend the type of planting in the area that was previously only water lilies. A variety of water plants, some above-head height, are now used in some of the margin areas and produce a more lively and three-dimensional display.

A lack of drawings at Longwood can make it difficult to attribute specific work to Shepheard. Drawings produced for the Idea Garden are clearly his, but the original proposals were by his predecessor, Thomas Church. What exists at Longwood today is similar in concept to Shepheard's vision, but not fully realized. More comprehensive is the work at the 650-foot-long Flower Garden Walk, one of the most popular features at Longwood. Although impressive, this was not Shepheard's favorite. He said that Longwood "tried to wipe people's eyes with displays of bedding plants."[23] Church had previously designed a small group of specialist gardens at the other end of the avenue. In 1977 Shepheard's improving hand gave a proper focal point to the other end of the walk. An existing Italian marble semicircular bench, known as the whispering bench, was moved twenty-five feet forward. A background screen of clipped hornbeam acted like a theatre curtain behind the bench. To the front, the single-path access was split, and a grass area was added between the split paths. This served to increase the scale of space, but it also spread the visitors to the sides so the main feature, the seat and hedge, could be seen from the axis. The new path layout had originally been a Church proposal of some years before, which Shepheard incorporated into his work.[24]

There were a number of unrealized projects in Philadelphia as well as for Central Park in New York. Two commissions are worth noting for their distinct differences. In Williamsburg, Virginia, Shepheard designed an inner courtyard, the Western Garden, for the Wallace Decorative Arts

Gallery (1983–1986). He found the idea of the museum fascinating: American and British furniture of the same period was exhibited together. The courtyard has typical Shepheard spatial control and details. It is a composition of rectangles, with stone paths and contrasting edges. The planting is soft and informal, in contrast to the structural form. The raised water basin is shallow, but uses a vegetable dye to increase the reflective qualities and to give a greater sense of depth. This is something that he could never convince Longwood to do with their fountains. In contrast to the museum, Emanuel Court (1988), at Twenty-second and Chestnut streets in Philadelphia, appears small and insignificant. Yet it exhibits all of Shepheard's design qualities and ideas. An easily missed urban space, Emanuel's Court is on a corner of a neo-Gothic-style converted church property. A mature American elm anchors the corner. Shepheard located a new path and seating area as an entrance access to the offices. It is reminiscent of his Goldsmith's site in London; here he located seating between the buttresses of the church, giving a sense of individual spaces. To the side of the main path, the area was completely planted, mostly with herbaceous plants. Shepheard said that he had difficulty both in convincing the owners to use herbaceous plants and in finding the right plants for the job— since herbaceous plants were hardly used in the United States. Although his love of water posed a problem in an exposed urban site, he managed to incorporate a large, flattish stone. He referred to it as a scraggy-looking boulder. A hole drilled through it and a recirculating pump has maintained a subtle flow of water for fifteen years. Shepheard almost completely abandoned the strong geometry that is apparent in his other work, but he still achieved a balanced and sensitive composition. He said that this was "a nice little garden that I was particularly pleased with. It's exactly what an urban garden should be like. You go in and the traffic is roaring away outside, but it's quiet, it's wonderful."[25]

There are indications of change or reinvention in his approach to design. What was starting to appear as a formulaic approach to design took a different direction. At Bessborough Gardens (1984) in London, Shepheard rationalized a complex interchange of roads into an informal London-type square. While there was a strong diagonal footpath across the square that led to a fountain, the other paths were decidedly informal and a move away from his previous work. There was more in common with the eighteenth century landscape ideals of Brown—a composition of sky, trees, and landforms—than there was with modernism. However, function played a key part in the design by providing a semienclosed and safe area from the surrounding traffic, an area of escape and refuge, but on a larger scale than Emanuel's Court. At Winfield House (1983), the American ambassador's residence in Regent's Park, Shepheard responded to the ideal of the English stately home and garden. He picks up the formal axis, extends it, and surrounds it with the most traditional of herbaceous borders and rose gardens. There are differences, and some Shepheard details show through in the paving and the rake on the clipped yew hedges around the rose garden. This was originally done to celebrate President Reagan's visit to London; most of the planting has now been replaced, although the spatial forms are much as Shepheard originally designed them.

It is in one of his last landscape projects that he was able to indulge his love of art, literature, plants, and design. Charleston House (1984–1985), in the Sussex Downs, is the only restoration project by Shepheard. As a landscape, it is essentially unknown and minor; however, its connection to the people who developed and used it give a level of importance. As the summer home of Vanessa Bell and Duncan Grant—part of the Bloomsbury group—it reflects a period of time in art, literature, and social ideals. Shepheard's drawings show his traditional strong geometry, but the reality is anything but that. His use of plants provided the perfect casual English country garden, quite unlike anything he had done previously. He delighted in this project for it gave him the opportunity to re-create the garden through the painting and writings associated with the owners and such visitors to Charleston as Virginia Woolf, Lytton Stratchey, and Maynard Keynes. Shepheard referred to them as a hedonistic lot and said, "Where else would you have such good company and conversation, fine wine and food, and a wonderful garden to make love in?"[26] His reference to Charleston provides an appropriate summary of his idea of a garden and landscape; it has purpose and form, but it is also to be enjoyed. Shepheard was a great admirer of Thomas Church, and one can see his principles within Shepheard's work. Church stated that there were no rules or "musts" in a garden, but that gardens will be "shaped by the desires of people who expect to find happiness in their gardens."[27] What Shepheard followed was Church's dictum that gardens are places for people first, a principle that is consistent throughout his career as illustrator, architect, planner, and landscape architect.[28]

Edward M. Bennis, ASLA, is the head of the School of Landscape at Manchester Metropolitan University and a consultant on historic parks and gardens. He has lectured internationally and conducted research work for English Heritage, regional governments, and the European Union.

NOTES

1 David Jacques, "Landscapes and Gardens in Britain 1930-2000," paper for the Garden History Society and the Twentieth Century Society, 27–28 March 1998, p. 2.

2 English Heritage is part of the Department of the Environment. There are separate registers for Scotland, Wales, and Northern Ireland.

3 Listed structures (buildings, walls, gateposts, signs, telephone boxes, etcetera) are protected within law, and special planning approval is required for repair, alterations, and removals. In terms of parks and gardens, there is no statutory or legal protection for those landscapes. While consideration will be given to the effect of any proposal that requires planning permissions to those landscapes, it is a gray area within the law.

4 Edward Bennis and John Dyke carried out the full survey for Cheshire in 1995. This was followed with the first stage of the survey for Lancashire. In both counties more than 400 landscapes were initially identified; approximately fifteen sites in each county were shortlisted for further detailed research.

5 Charles Birnbaum of the National Park Service calls this a soft dateline as compared to the American hard dateline where landscapes cannot be included.

6 American Military Cemetery (Olmsted Brothers); Barbara Hepworth Sculpture Garden (Dame Barbara Hepworth); Commonwealth Institute (Dame Sylvia Crowe); Friarwood Valley (G.W. Grubb); Harlow Water Garden (Sir Frederick Gibbard); Harvey's Roof Garden (Sir Geoffrey Jellicoe); The House (Sir Frederick Gibbard); Plymouth Physic Garden (Sir Geoffrey Jellicoe); Queen's Park (Swindon Borough Architect); St. Catherine's College (Arne Jacobson); The Vale, Edgbaston (Mary Mitchell with Cason and Condor); Wakall Memorial (Sir Geoffrey Jellicoe).

7 "Getting It All Together," *Building*, June 1980, 37.

8 From Peter Shepheard's files, a file copy of a letter to Lady Goldsmith dated 6 September 1946, three pages of notes titled "Somerhill—notes on the garden plans," and an untitled rough sketch.

9 Annabel Downs, unpublished interviews from November 1999 to January 2000, p. 53, in Landscape Institute Archives, London.

10 Edward Bennis, interview from February 2000.

11 S. Harvey and S. Rettig, eds., *Fifty Years of Landscape Design* (London: The Landscape Press, 1985).

12 Peter Shepheard, *Modern Gardens* (London: The Architectural Press, 1954), p. 74.

13 Downs, p. 54.

14 Jan Birkstead, *Relating Architecture to Landscape* (London: E. & F.N. Spon, 1999), p. 74.

15 *Modern Gardens*, p. 14.

16 The introduction to *Modern Gardens* was recently reprinted in *Relating Architecture to Landscape*; Birkstead refers to it as a forward-looking text.

17 Shepheard taught at Penn for numerous short periods. He was Dean of the Faculty of Arts from 1971 to 1979. He continued as a partner in his London practice during this period.

18 Downs, p. 62.

19 Bennis, p. 4.

20 Landscape Development Plan (Philadelphia: Center for Environmental Design, Graduate School of Fine Arts, University of Pennsylvania, 1977), p. 2. Shepheard credits nineteen graduate students and lists eight deputy directors of the project. Colin Franklin and Laurie Olin are credited with the perspectives.

21 This observation was made in general of Shepheard's work and published as part of his obituary by Alan Powers, *The Independent*, 20 April 2002.

22 It was a cross between *Victoria cruziana* and *Victoria amazonica*, produced by Pat Nutt, who supervised the site works on the lily pools for Shepheard.

23 Bennis, p. 13.

24 Notes by Shepheard from a meeting 10 November 1977, in the Architectural Archives, University of Pennsylvania, Philadelphia.

25 Bennis, pp. 15-16. The garden is very well maintained, although the benches and the adjoining planters have been removed.

26 Bennis, interview on 2 March 2000.

27 Thomas Church, *Gardens Are for People* (Berkeley: University of California Press, 1995, third ed.), p. 6.

28 Shepheard held many positions in his professional career: president of the RIBA, the Landscape Institute, the Architectural Association, and the Master Art Workers Guild. He was a member of the RTPI and was knighted in 1980. He died 11 April 2002, aged eighty-eight, one week after the Wave Hill conference.

The Origin of the Landscape Architecture Profession in Portugal during the Modern Movement

Cristina Castel-Branco

Figure 1. Gulbenkian Foundation garden, Lisbon, Portugal, 1969: Its design reflects a change in man's attitude to the environment, the concern for the existing natural processes. (All photographs, Cristina Castel-Branco)

The title of this conference announces a proactive and ambitious intent. It not only advises us to study modern landscape expressions, it also challenges us to make them more visible and preserve them. We are asked to analyze the essence of the modern expression in the landscape and defend it relentlessly.

Two books in a series of biographies of eminent modern European landscape architects, edited by Ken Fieldhouse and published by the Landscape Design Trust, were instrumental to my research for this paper: one, on Francisco Caldeira Cabral; the other, on Sir Geoffrey Jellicoe. To understand the spaces designed forty years ago, I also toured modern gardens and parks in Portugal, observing them at different times of the day and carefully noting their maturing character, their use, and the design solutions that created them.

During my research I came to appreciate the value of the modern heritage in Portugal and its strong link with painting and sculpture and the new sciences of ecology and sociology. But I have to admit that the method for selecting and preserving the best is still an open question for me. In my previous academic experience with gardens from the sixteenth to the nineteenth century, time was the best judge for selecting the masterpieces. A succession of judges through the generations attributed value to the best, to the ones considered real jewels by their owners or the public. As for modern landscape architecture, not enough time has passed to filter the many works of the postwar period. What processes, what criteria should be used to choose the ones deserving preservation? Or should they all be preserved? Should the selection be made by the critics, assisted by the designers of the modern works themselves?

Although professionals have considered the selection process, for me the question remains without a clear answer. But for the works of previous centuries the attribution of value has been directly linked to the qualities of a place and the strength of its design meaning. Frequently the designer left this meaning subtle or even hidden. It nags at the visitor with bits and pieces of a message that can be decoded only after carefully putting together a puzzle made up of pieces of art, nature, and time. I have become more and more convinced that to preserve the modern heritage it is essential to understand its time and, even more important, the meaning of the new created space, the hidden meaning, the message effected by the outpouring of the designer's creative process. One might say that this approach would be appropriate for all centuries and for any work of art, but let us try to use it in examining the design of the modern movement.

The Postwar Historical Moment Just as Versailles was the product of the social and political structure of absolutism, the modern

Figure 2. The Gulbenkian Foundation museum cantilevers over the lake.

movement is the product of the two major wars of the century. During World War I an incubation period began. Painters, poets, and composers launched the avant-garde in a new quest that would become the modern movement. After World War II the creative avant-garde included architects and landscape architects who became both actors and tools expressing the new concerns, collective knowledge, and emotions of this new society they called modern.

Painters best illustrate the links between art and the social moment. The linkages of the first period, during World War I, were clearly expressed by Paul Klee early in 1915, when he recorded in his diary these significant words: "The more horrifying this world becomes the more art becomes abstract."[1] In 1931 Klee went on to teach at the Bauhaus and his work became an influential theoretical formulation of modern art, best expressed in his book, *The Thinking Eye*.

In the second period, following World War II, landscape architects were at work as a new profession. Not only was art becoming more abstract, but social and ecological concerns were becoming inseparable from architectural input, a development noted by other artists and intellectuals. For example, referring to Cliveden, Jellicoe writes, "This little garden illustrates the change in man's attitude to environment that has taken place this century—from the nineteenth-century academic outlook to the ecological approach of the twentieth century."[2]

Portugal in the 1950s In her biography of Caldeira Cabral, Teresa Andresen emphasizes the war's direct influence on the profession: "Landscape architecture grew from those disturbed years." It is interesting to consider such a statement. Without such an event would Gropius have gone to the United States and Harvard University, where he influenced an entire generation of landscape architects, including Garret Eckbo, James Rose, and Dan Kiley?[3] Did this international event create a new relationship between art and nature? Where did Portugal stand? A small country of 10 million on the western tip of Europe, it had not entered the war. It remained neutral. This neutrality would have implications for landscape architecture in future years. Interestingly, our first landscape architect studied abroad, in Germany, from 1936 to 1939, just before World War II. His name—Francisco Caldeira Cabral—arouses in any Portuguese landscape architect the same reverence and admiration that the name of Frederick Law Olmsted inspires in American professionals. During Cabral's long lifetime he created (in 1941) and consolidated (until 1993) the profession of landscape architecture, expanding it from design to landscape planning.

From the end of the war until the end of the 1950s Portugal witnessed another disturbance, Salazar's dictatorial regime. For obvious reasons art critics have called it the "the decade of silence." Any threat to the status quo was brutally silenced. Artists and architects left to go abroad in their quest for the new and the genuine. Some settled in Paris, London, Milan, and Munich. One result was direct contact with new sources of information, for example the study of the New Town movement in 1956 by a young Portuguese architect, Viana Barreto, who was instrumental in the development of a new era in town planning in Lisbon.

A special event contributed to the advancement of the arts in Portugal during this time of adverse conditions. The wealthy oil magnate Calouste Gulbenkian donated his art collection to Portugal and created a foundation for the promotion of the arts. As Rui Mario Goncalves points out, "The situation, more and more tense, did not get worse thanks to the raising of a new force, which appeared as a miracle: the creation of the Gulbenkian Foundation in 1956."[4] The architecture of the headquarters was designed with a strong relationship to the garden surrounding it, and both became reference points in Portugal's modern movement. Since then the Gulbenkian Foundation has been a pillar of the arts in Portugal.

Movement and Time   In the design realm, a rich source of influence was Geoffrey Jellicoe, a friend of Cabral's from 1956. As we learn from his biography, Jellicoe's intellectual interest in the essence of landscape architecture as a design profession led him to consider the new ideas about space and time being developed by physicists and philosophers:

Behind Appearance by C.H. Waddington was a great resource to Jellicoe's study of modern painting. If a landscape designer were

to have only one book on the subject, Jellicoe felt that Waddington's should be it. Waddington, himself a scientist, related modern scientific theories to the work of modern painters. Many of the ideas about space-time and the role of the subconscious which appear in Jellicoe's writing and design can be found in this book.[5]

Waddington writes, "Space which has been considered timeless is actually inseparable from motion which involves time."[6] And Einstein's theories revealed that there is no way of determining which of multiple frames involving space in motion and in time provides a correct measurement. Jellicoe was interested in how these new theories of space-time as explored by modern artists pertain to landscape design. For example, he considered the work of Burle Marx as having been designed for people in motion: "It is not only that the lines of the gardens are rhythmic in themselves, but they seem to be so partly in response to movement in the beholder, a symptom of the restless energy of the age in which we live."[7]

Perhaps the fourth dimension is best revealed through landscape design. Movement makes perceivable the dimension of time, and in a garden landscape architects design the space for people in movement. On a large scale, the growth of plant material encapsulates long periods of time in annual wood rings, in increasing volume, in lichens covering the bark of old trees. On a medium scale, the expression of seasonal cycles in gardens gives man the measure of annual time. And on a daily scale, even shadows are a register of time shed on the space of the garden.

In Jellicoe's work movement was a conscious element in the design process—similar to a kinetic work by Naum Gabo that Jellicoe describes as one that "moves within itself changing the space relation of the parts." According to Jellicoe, the role of kinetic sculpture in the landscape is not to compete with the movement of the natural world, but "to draw our attention to this more subtle layer of motion."[8]

How is all this perceivable in the design of the Gulbenkian Foundation's garden by Cabral's young disciples, Viana Barreto and Ribeiro Telles? The paths allow the visitor with the maximum number of possibilities for movement. The grading and layout of the concrete stepped ramps create the sense of a much deeper space; a serpentine path offers a profusion of frames as the visitor moves through the garden, giving a special experience of time that contrasts with the still view from the sitting areas within walls of vegetation where both the visitor and time seem to stop. Comparing Cabral's early designs with the work of his first graduates in landscape design, we realise how much the master was still rooted in the premodern style. His formal design approach prepared

Figure 3. The Gulbenkian Foundation auditorium creates an intense dialogue between architecture and garden.

Figure 4. Olivais Park, Lisbon, 1960: The Valley of Silence by M. Sousa da Câmara is a solid, long-lasting design using native vegetation.

Figure 5. In Olivais a three-dimensional soft design in the pavement of the cobblestone plaza reminds us of Noguchi's work for the Chase Manhattan Bank Plaza in New York City.

the space as one framed landscape for sitting and for contemplating. His students readily absorbed the modern elements and intuitively designed with them. Later, Cabral produced dynamic spaces, but the first modern innovators were A. Barreto, G.R. Telles, and architect Alvaro Dentinho.

Space Writing about Cliveden, Jellicoe describes the "desire for the expansion of space which is of peculiar relevance to landscape art: Just as movements like ripples on the surface of water could go on indefinitely if only there were no obstructions, so there was a desire on the part of artists of all kinds to break through a boundary, whether that of a hedge, a building, or a picture frame."[9] The Gulbenkian garden meanders around the building, which in turn cantilevers its concrete structures over the water and plants to create a sense of expansion. The concert wall rising from the water sends its vertical lines into an endless dimension. The link between building and garden is achieved by the introduction of patios, open spaces inside the building, and sculpture that expands from the inside of the large hall out through the glass into the garden.

The Subconscious in Landscape Art A multitude of coincidental forces (the war, advancing physics research on time and space, the applied consequences of the social studies) all influenced the essence of the artistic process, whether in music, painting, or landscape architecture. Klee uses a metaphorical comparison to capture the way that culture influences the artist:

> The artist has busied himself with this multiform world and in some measure got his bearings in it, quietly, all by himself. He is so well oriented that he can put order into the flux of phenomena and experiences. This sense of direction in nature and life,

this branching and spreading array, I shall compare with the root of the tree. From the root the sap rises up into the artist, flows through him, flows to his eye. He is the trunk of the tree. Overwhelmed and activated by the force of the current, he conveys his vision into his work. In full view of the world, the crown of the tree unfolds and spreads in time and in space, and so with his work. And yet, standing at his appointed place, as the trunk of the tree, he does nothing other than gather and pass on what rises from the depths. He neither serves nor commands—he transmits. His position is humble. And the beauty at the crown is not his own; it has merely passed through him.[10]

The creative process is rooted in the subconscious. Modernists assumed it, and Jellicoe was aware of it. Throughout his writings on modern painting and landscape design he refers to the power of the subconscious both to inspire design and to heighten the experience of the viewer. As he writes, "We can and should make landscape as meaningful as painting."[11]

The Forces at Work in Portugal during the Modern Movement In Portugal the modern movement coincided with the beginning of the profession of landscape architecture, which embraced both project design and landscape planning. Introduced by Caldeira Cabral, the first degree in landscape architecture was offered at the Lisbon School of Agronomy in 1940. With his German education, Cabral based his teaching in an engineering school (agronomy and forestry), emphasizing the benefits of the cross-fertilization of art and science to produce a sound and responsible design in the landscape. At the beginning, the profession was based on ecological design principles, a movement that was to gain an influence in the professional world then dominated by architects and engineers. During the 1950s, the first generation of Portuguese landscape architects thus became missionaries of a cause difficult to implement: to speak the design language of architects while applying ecological principles in proposed solutions. This was difficult because they were designing with nature in a modern movement that typically didn't embrace context.

Along with his first disciples, Cabral successfully launched a new profession and gained the respect of other professions in the design and planning market. Observed from a distance of fifty years, it seems as if the professor sent that first generation of landscape architects in five directions with each of his best students personalizing specific tasks in a multidisciplinary profession: design, applied ecology, landscape heritage, planning, and nature conservation. Urban projects were becoming available in the capital at that time, providing fresh opportunities for the contribution of landscape architects. Arranged under these five headings, modern examples of landscape architecture in Lisbon have survived the test of time to become references for the profession. The landscape architects were Ribeiro Telles, A. Viana Barreto, M. Sousa da Cãmara, Alvaro Dentinho, and J. Marques Moreira, and the works range from gardens to urban parks. Cabral also personally made a firm contribution in each of these five fields of work. By the 1960s he had become the president of IFLA, and his contacts with Jellicoe, René Pechere, Sylvia Crowe, Lawrence Halprin, and Lewis Mumford were a permanent stimulus for the up-dating of the design and planning practice in Portugal.

I shall now briefly consider three Lisbon landmark works. First, the headquarters of the Gulbenkian Foundation, designed by Telles and Barreto, is an excellent example of a modern Portuguese landscape architectural masterpiece. Second, Olivais was a first attempt at a garden city, with sixty percent of the space surrounding an International Style residential area in an expanding neighborhood of Lisbon. Here for the first time, landscape architects were brought in at the beginning to help integrate solutions for a planned urban residential development. Olivais was a joint effort of young landscape architects Dentinho and Sousa da Cãmara, the latter also responsible for a watershed park, an application of ecological principles with design solutions that proved very successful with the local population. Third, Barreto's waterfront design surrounding Belèm, a historic sixteenth-century tower at the river entrance has proved to be a very successful modern public space.

The Gulbenkian Foundation At Gulbenkian the designers almost instinctively made visible Jellicoe's wish "to make landscape as meaningful as painting." Their creation was cross-fertilized by artistic issues of movement in space, ecology and time, the modern design and materials of the building, and a poetic vision of a sixteenth-century paradise. Recently asked by his students about the secret of his work, Telles revealed that underlying his design was the episode of the "island of love" in an epic poem by Camões that describes the discovery of paradise during journeys to India. This romantic approach did not, however, prevent the designers from binding their proposal to the modern concrete building. Telles and Barreto describe "the search for a total and intimate relation between the elements which create the whole, embracing in the composition all the available area in a way that the life of the building itself would spread naturally to the outdoor space. In return the garden would penetrate into the building's inside."[12]

The Gulbenkian Foundation was not just a center for the arts; the architecture was in itself a sculpture in the landscape. Telles's search for paradise and perfection became a vision for the garden as a complete harmony of water, sky, and trees offered as a gift to humanity. The public has understood this vision, and the park is used every hour of the day as a haven from the city. A large buffer of poplars and grading provides almost full isolation from the surrounding buildings.

Just as Klee refused to believe that a work of art could be projected automatically from the unconscious, so, we are told by his biographer, "Jellicoe first resolved the practical issues before creating the hidden message. Often the hidden theme came to him during the process of working out programmatic elements."[13] Here is an important point for our analysis of modern Portuguese landscape expressions. Natural processes are complex issues that require a full understanding, from the behavior of water and wind to the knowledge of plant material as it grows and blooms. All these processes involve an intricate system of relationships, much more complicated than painting and sculpture, poetry and music. For the landscape architect the process of gestation is complex, involving observation, meditation, and finally a technical mastery of pictorial and natural elements. The background of scientific and design issues must be solid. At the Gulbenkian Foundation, the grading, the location of the pond, and the drainage of the whole garden were taken into account and creatively incorporated into the design. According to Telles, "movement was translated by growth, by the volumes' alteration, color, and light of plant material through the seasons, by the development of the park, by the presence of fauna that required protection, through water movement launched toward the lake, and by the human presence."[14]

Olivais The same principles of mastering the technical elements, reaching the subconscious, and then allowing the vision to emerge from

Figure 6. *Torre de Belèm, Lisbon: a sixteenth-century building surrounded by a modern design by A. Viana Barreto, 1967*

Figure 7. *Torre de Belèm: The strength of the design resides in a curving line surrounding the tower.*

the nature of the landscape in its original form are evident in another work of 1960. M. Sousa da Cãmara, a young landscape architect who was called in by urban planners J. Botelho and Carlos Duarte to complete the design team, would apply and adjust the concepts of Ebeneezer Howard to the Lisbon development of Olivais. The watershed nine-hectare park was the surviving small green lung of 189 hectares developed to house a mixed population of middle-class and low-income residents.[15] A strict budget and tight construction rules resulted in small apartments built in seven-story buildings. The population of 40,000 residents was given a generous amount of open space, piazzas, playgrounds, pedestrian walks, and other outdoor solutions to take advantage of the mild Lisbon climate and compensate from the limited indoor living space.

In this environment Cãmara was able to create a solid, long-lasting design by draining the major water line, thus creating a clearing, offering paths for movement, and protecting the inside of the park, called the Valley of Silence, with a thick line of umbrella pines. In this case, not only were aesthetic and ecological issues the bases of the design, but social concerns were also at the forefront of some of the solutions. The landscape had to serve a low-income residential area, a consideration that influenced the simple design and ornament and minimalist solutions in which native vegetation played a significant role, both for its reliable adaptation and low maintenance costs. Cãmara elegantly solved the problem of cross-circulation without using paths that cut up the valley. A thick edge with a variety of trees—umbrella pines, judas trees, and curtains of poplars—intercepted the wind that carried the pollution of industrial fumes and dusts. The small areas surrounded by apartment buildings were designed to encourage a rich tissue of urban relationships. The informal layout of the buildings allowed for a close planting of trees. Since the trees (poplars, plane trees, and cypresses) reached to the top of the seven-story structures, it seems today as if the design only allowed buildings to be as tall as the trees.

Landscape architects were called on to be part of the technical team to design the small plazas and playgrounds and the pedestrian network around the buildings. Open areas outnumbered building areas, and in some cases interesting modern designs were developed for the plazas by Dentinho. Although maintenance is not as high as that at the Gulbenkian Foundation, some of the designs show clear links to modern expressions, for example the cobblestone plaza where a sculpture in the pavement reminds us of the Noguchi work for the Chase Manhattan Bank Plaza in New York. While the Olivais Plaza is poorly maintained, it is visible in its three-dimensional, soft design. The traditional Portuguese calçada (repeated in Rio de Janeiro by Burle Marx) conveys the special atmosphere of Lisbon, where modern landscape architects have used it extensively as a design medium. An original playground was designed in two tall concrete circles, like two fortresses linked by a bridge. Today, in an abandoned state without equipment, it still offers an original and interesting design solution.

Belèm The tower of Belèm has been sitting at the mouth of the river for some four hundred years, defending the entrance to Lisbon harbour. Its symbolic location and appearance are so strong that any design had to submit to it. Viana Barreto worked with the large scale of the Tagus River and reduced modern expression to the minimal level, allowing the tower to play its major role. The strength of the design resides in a curving line surrounding the tower that recedes and creates an amphitheatre of low steps that is simple but in magnificent dialogue with the river. The design emphasizes a visual axis toward the land, directing the view to a chapel on the hill from which the caravels were spotted when safely coming into habour. The strong intention of this twentieth-century modern green axis shows a clear relationship between the two old monuments. The natural process of tidal movement is taken advantage of in a subtle solution that retains water around the base of the tower even at low tide. The reflective nature of this surface maintains the visual association with its original context. A simple lawn completes the design with clusters of surrounding umbrella pines that open to the axial space. The touristic and social use of this space makes it a success.

Strategies for ongoing preservation and management of the modern heritage created during the twentieth century are currently not a high priority for the authorities in charge. Gradually, information about these works is being published, but, unfortunately, the recent emphasis has been more on the ecological service of landscape architects and less on the contribution of these works as examples of art that represents the beginning of a profession in Portugal during the modern movement.

Cristina Castel-Branco has been a professor of landscape architecture at the University of Lisbon (UTL) since 1989. From 1993 to 2002 she was project director for the restoration of the Botanic Garden of Ajuda. Practicing with Victor Walker, she designs new and restores old gardens.

Figure 8. At Torre de Belèm a simple lawn with umbrella pines completes the design.

NOTES

1 Herbert Read, *A Concise History of Modern Painting* (New York: Frederick A. Praeger, 1999), p. 180.

2 Ken Fieldhouse, *Geoffrey Jellicoe* (Surrey: Landscape Design Trust, 1998), p. 81.

3 Teresa L. Andresen, *Francisco Caldeira Cabral* (Surrey: Landscape Design Trust, 2001), p. 34.

4 Rui Mario Goncalves, *Arte Portuguesa nos Anos 50* (Lisbon: C.M. Beja and Fundacao Calouste Gulbenkian, 1992), p. 88.

5 *Geoffrey Jellicoe*, p. 77.

6 C.H. Waddington, *Behind Appearance* (Edinburgh: University Press, 1969), quoted in *Geoffrey Jellicoe*, p. 13.

7 Geoffrey Jellicoe, *Studies in Landscape Design* (Oxford: Oxford University Press, 1960), p. 106.

8 Ibid., p. 105.

9 Ibid.

10 Paul Klee, *Theorie de l'Art Moderne* (Paris: Desnoel, 1985), pp. 16–17.

11 Jellicoe, *Studies in Landscape Design*, p. 76.

12 Goncalo R. Telles and Antonio V Barreto in *Revista Arquitectura*, 1969, 212.

13 *Geoffrey Jellicoe*, p. 93.

14 Telles, p. 217.

15 Ana Tostões, Os Verdes anos, FAUP publicaçoes, Porto, p. 76.

The Last Landscape

Richard Longstreth

Figure 1. Shoppers' World shopping center, Framingham, Massachusetts, 1949–1951; Ketchum, Gina & Sharp, architects; Arthur Shurcliff, landscape architect; demolished 1994 (Longstreth, 1988)

Figure 2. Connecticut General Life Insurance Company offices, Bloomfield, Connecticut, 1956-1957; Skidmore, Owings & Merrill, architects and landscape architects (Longstreth, 2000)

Landscapes of the recent past are, too often, the last considered and the most threatened. As nearly the last things we have done, they are often the first things we believe must be done again. The last landscape frequently is cast as one of errors, functional and esthetic, before it has had the time to acquire a substantial past of its own.[1] From the preservation perspective, no greater challenge exists. But it is a challenge worth addressing for a number of reasons.

The basic arguments are essentially the same for preserving both architecture and landscape architecture of the recent past, which, for purposes of discussion here, is limited to the three decades following World War II. First, this period benefited from a stunning array of artistic talent, with the maturing of pioneer modernists and the emergence of a new generation as well. Thomas Church, Garrett Eckbo, Paul Friedberg, Lawrence Halprin, Dan Kiley, Hideo Sasaki, and Robert Zion are among the figures who created designs of extraordinary character that received widespread recognition nationally and internationally when they were created. The post-World War II legacy is at least as strong as any other period in landscape architecture from the standpoint of conceptual originality and formal sophistication.

Second—and this is an aspect that many landscape architects recognize instinctively, but is less obvious among architects and others involved in preservation—the period was one of enormous innovation in settlement patterns when the fundamental nature of metropolitan structure experienced dramatic changes. The extent of low-density, decentralized, and eventually also polycentric forms of development became much more pronounced than had previously been the case. The United States was by far the most important crucible for these changes, and landscape design played a central role in many instances, for it was the setting that established the ambient character so essential to the appeal of such places as alternatives to the urban norm.

A primary manifestation of this shift was the regional shopping mall, whose creators sought to bring the advantages of the centralized business configuration downtown within easy reach of middle-class households that now lay near the urban periphery. The result, of course, was anything but urban in character. The initial archetype for the mall was in fact the then-prevailing idealized view of "ye olde" New England town green, the appeal of which lay as much in a purported capacity to foster social interaction as in its bucolic character.[2]

As the shopping-mall idea took hold, these places became an important proving ground for applying new ideas in landscape architecture to the public realm. Even with budget constraints, as Sidney Shurcliff complained about at Shoppers' World near Framingham, Massachusetts

(1948–1951), complexes with copious amount of central open space afforded a then-rare opportunity to adapt some of the new ideas introduced in private gardens to a larger scale and broader use (Figure 1).[3] Lawrence Halprin produced one of the most fully developed and sophisticated examples for Old Orchard Shopping Center, northwest of Chicago (1954–1956), where the concept of an informal, but highly active interplay of form and space was carried into the layout of the complex itself.[4] But there were many other, less adventurous manifestations such as Parole Plaza near Annapolis, Maryland (1960-1962), where the concept of bringing the garden into the marketplace was nonetheless crucial to establishing the character of the complex from a marketing no less than an aesthetic standpoint.

A second major sphere of innovation was the suburban corporate headquarters, or what is called the corporate estate, where a function that had been key to defining the city center since the mid-nineteenth century experienced a pronounced shift, assuming the mode of a great country place.[5] Often the work of renowned architects and landscape architects and repositories of noteworthy assemblages of art, these latter-day villas were not, however, completely private bastions. In some cases, as with the Connecticut General Life Insurance Company near Hartford, Connecticut, by Skidmore, Owings & Merrill (1956-1957), their grounds were readily accessible to the public and played a significant role in defining place amid the low-density residential tracts that lay around them (Figure 2).[6] Connecticut General was a seminal work in this regard, one that had a profound impact on the conceptualization of such places for several decades. Even more famous is the park Sasaki designed to complement Eero Saarinen's John Deere headquarters in Moline, Illinois, completed in 1964.[7] In both examples, the picturesque English park of the late eighteenth and early nineteenth centuries provided the conceptual springboard, but the designs are essentially new in their breadth and simplicity of effect. At the same time, when compared to contemporaneous designs for shopping malls, these schemes underscore the multifaceted nature of landscape architecture of the period and the ability of the profession to respond in new, creative ways to essential differences in programmatic demands.

The third sphere, and certainly others could be added, is residential development. Some very innovative work existed in this realm in terms of site design and the treatment of individual properties. Hollin Hills in Fairfax County, Virginia, developed largely during the 1950s, is a prime example. For a large subdivision it was unusual in its respect for the terrain and existing woodlands as well as for its uncompromisingly modern houses. Several landscape architects contributed to the scheme over

Figure 3. Hollin Hills residential development, Fairfax County, Virginia, begun 1946; Robert Davenport, developer; Charles M. Goodman, architect; Lou Bernard Voight, Dan Kiley, and Eric Paepcke, landscape architects (Longstreth, 2001)

Figure 4. Bowie residential development, Prince George's County, Maryland, begun 1957; Levitt & Sons, developers, designers, and builders (Longstreth, 2000)

time, including a young Dan Kiley.[8] The ecological concerns nascent at Hollin Hills became a formative component of the Sea Ranch, begun in the mid-1960s and one of the most innovative residential enclaves to be realized in the United States during the twentieth century. Here Halprin and his architect-collaborators, MLTW, developed a dynamic and decisively new approach to relate buildings and landscape—an approach that continues to resonate as a model for rural development.[9] There are probably more distinguished, singular postwar residential developments than we realize in the United States, but they nonetheless remain very much the exception.

The mainstream generally did not involve architects or landscape architects of note, but the results also beg our attention. At no time in American history was the opportunity so prevalent for so many people to obtain a slice of the American dream, a freestanding single-family house with a copious yard. For millions of Americans, many of whom were just entering the middle class, postwar housing tracts represented a seminal change in their living environment.[10] They also represented a seminal shift in metropolitan structure, the full effects of which we are only beginning to comprehend. The Levitt-developed community of Bowie near Washington, D.C., begun in the late 1950s, is a good example of many tracts where site design remained an important attribute. What occurred in such cases was a skilled adaptation of naturalistic planning principles that had been refined in the layout of elite suburbs prior to World War II to more constrained circumstances (Figure 4). The mass-produced approach to residential development that Levitt was instrumental in advancing was often the subject of derision among professionals and critics alike, but from the consumer's standpoint these tracts represented nirvana, and as they mature it is imperative to take fresh stock of their considerable merits. They are nonrenewable resources where the landscape more than the buildings defined the character of place.

The framework presented thus far contributes to arguments for significance, but what about the need for preservation? Some observers see all the attention on the recent past as artificially rushing the process, but they ignore the fundamental reality that many components of the recent past are seriously threatened. Shoppers' World is gone. Old Orchard is remodeled. Connecticut General is seriously threatened, and in any event it is unlikely that its bucolic landscape will survive whatever the outcome. Sea Ranch's pathbreaking site plan was changed years ago. The Bowies of the nation survive underappreciated and sometimes vilified, their value as habitat ignored or snubbed in many circles. In a society that continues to experience substantial growth as well as change and one

that is ever more prone to disposability, we can no longer afford to wait for two or three generations to elapse before we focus on preserving things.

From this standpoint, a few types of landscape design seem reasonably safe. The museum garden is one example, but even these can be subject to change when the significance of their design is not fully understood or appreciated. A good example is afforded by Philip Johnson's Roofless Church in New Harmony, Indiana (1960), which has always been under the tutelage of a foundation. The importance of this design, at least as a work of architecture, is understood, but in recent years the main interior court, which was predominantly paved, has been altered to one that is primarily lawn, markedly changing the effect and the relationship between this space and the fields beyond.

The same fragility holds true for private gardens. The original owners almost always remain superb stewards, but when the property changes hands, the garden is often the first thing to be altered or even destroyed. Perhaps it is just neglected, but the impact can be much the same. Gardens are very personal things, and that special relationship increases their fragility in the long term. Many of the postwar era are lost.

The public park might seem a safer realm. Historically changes to such places tended to be made in increments over time, and often those changes are now seen as contributing to the richness of the whole. Even changes deemed less than enhancing have tended to be piecemeal and generally reversible. But today, change seems to be more comprehensive and final: The existing landscape is eradicated and an entirely new scheme put in its place. Such has been the case in recent years with Sasaki's Copley Plaza in Boston (1966) and also with Dan Kiley's block at Independence Mall in Philadelphia (1963). Both were lauded projects in their day; both became cast as liabilities by the next generation; both will never have a chance for reassessment with lives of less than forty years.

Such decisive change is often justified on the basis of functional obsolescence. Kiley's portion of Independence Mall, for example, was hampered by two other blocks of less sophisticated design, and most of the ensemble served little purpose. The Kiley block was a superb design by all accounts, but it never had a user constituency, and the siting was a disaster.

The challenge of function looms large with many projects of the recent past, none more pointedly than the urban mall. Pedestrian ways such as those which Victor Gruen and Garrett Eckbo designed at Fresno, California, were seen as a cure for decline in central business districts, making the core again competitive with shopping malls on the periphery (Figure 5).[11] More recently, however, these projects have been cast as

Figure 5. Fulton Mall, Fresno, California, 1960–1964; Victor Gruen Associates, architects; Garrett Eckbo, landscape architect (Longstreth, 1972)

Figure 6. Constitution Plaza, Hartford, Connecticut, 1959–1963; Charles DuBose, architect; Sasaki, Walker Associates, landscape architects; various architects for individual buildings (Longstreth, 2002)

Figure 7. Capital Park residential development, Washington, D.C., 1959–1963; Satterlee & Smith, architects; Dan Kiley, landscape architect (Longstreth, 2002)

Figure 8. Washington Square East (Society Hill) redevelopment area, realized design begun late 1950s; Edmund Bacon and others, planners; Collins, Adelman & Dutot, landscape architects; view of neighborhood park (Longstreth, 2002)

Figure 9. Community garden adjacent to 3901 Connecticut Avenue apartment house, Washington, D.C., begun as a Victory Garden ca. 1942, converted to ornamental garden ca. 1946, destroyed 1996 (Longstreth, 1995)

contributors to downtown's downward spiral. Citizens have generally applauded when their Main Streets have been reopened and all vestiges of malling disappeared. But should this scenario be universal? Calls for preserving the first executed example in the United States, designed in 1959 by Victor Gruen for Kalamazoo, Michigan, were unsuccessful, but it is doubtful that the modifications that ensued or, indeed, that any design solution in itself will bring life back to what has become a moribund area.[12] Could not some cases where the work is of interest, as with the first example realized for a town in Atchison, Kansas (1966), induce an alternative approach? Capitalizing on a now unusual and evocative environment, combined with a sound tenant structure and marketing strategy, to encourage revitalization is precisely what preservation has done with success on hundreds of Main Streets nationwide over the past twenty years. Malls can be successful in certain cases, especially in university towns. Examples by Halprin in Charlottesville, Virginia (1972–1975), and by architects Shapiro Petrauskas Gelber in Burlington, Vermont, are good illustrations of the fact that it is not the concept but the way in which it is developed and tied to the tastes of the community that is the crucial factor.

The urban plaza and other components of large-scale downtown urban-renewal complexes can pose more formidable challenges in terms of function. Charles Center in Baltimore, with a site plan that was a collaborative enterprise that included RTKL, Wallace McHarg Roberts & Todd, and Richard Potts, and Constitution Plaza by Sasaki, Walker and Associates in Hartford, both of the mid-to-late 1960s, are good examples of endeavors that were widely heralded in their day as catalysts to urban revitalization (Figure 6).[13] But much like the urban mall, their promise often went unfulfilled. Today terraces and other spaces conceived as magnets for human interaction are dismissed as forbidding places,

divorced from the street and from the city. In reality they tend to be little used except for passage, while incurring substantial maintenance and security bills. Should such work, which can now be assessed as having no small degree of historical significance in its own right, be the focus of preservation initiatives? Or should they be modified to render them more currently appealing for human use, a step that would almost certainly result in substantial physical change? These questions beg rigorous consideration and debate, for they are likely to arise soon and could easily succumb to opinions based on little more than emotion and expediency.

Urban-renewal projects also underscore the extent to which personal taste can affect change, for few enterprises are held in such low esteem today. Perhaps the most effective way of reshaping public opinion is to address first examples that pose little or no functional roadblocks and also have a built-in constituency. Upper-middle-class and middle-class residential districts such as Lake Meadows in Chicago, Lafayette Park in Detroit, the Southwest Washington Redevelopment Area, and Society Hill in Philadelphia are all good examples.[14] The Southwest Redevelopment Area was among the most ambitious of its kind, effectively transforming an entire precinct of the federal city to reflect avant-garde planning ideals of the mid-twentieth century. Mostly realized between 1960 and 1970, the tract boasted an array of row houses, mid-rise apartment complexes, churches, commercial facilities, cultural institutions, and parks (Figure 7).[15] Many of the best and brightest architects and landscape architects, including Sasaki and Kiley, contributed to what was seen as a demonstration project, exemplifying high standards applied to the public sphere. Despite some lapses in maintenance, little has changed in the precinct's physical fabric since it was completed. With a substantial number of residents who are enthusiastic about its extraordinary attributes, there is no reason why the entire area could not receive protection as a historic district.

Indeed, precisely that has occurred in Society Hill. While mostly venerated for its vast stock of eighteenth- and early nineteenth-century buildings, the district is also a benchmark in the history of preservation. Conceived by City Planning Commission director Edmund Bacon, the project was unprecedented in its scope and unusual in its concept. Bacon's strategy of marshalling a huge enclave of old buildings, many in poor—even derelict—condition, to serve as the basis for a sweeping revitalization effort designed to bring affluent households back to the city was nothing short of revolutionary at that time.[16] So too was his comprehensive scheme of compatible infrastructural improvements designed by Collins, Adelman & Dutot—street lights, sidewalks, and, most innovative, a series of interior pedestrian ways, varied in size and character, that would permeate the area and serve as nodes for human activity (Figure 8). This scheme, largely realized in the 1960s, now receives the same protection as the older components of the district, thanks to an enlightened policy implemented by the municipal preservation office a few years ago.

Underlying all the threats to the recent past is a lack of recognition. Few people outside the profession know so much as the names of leading landscape architects. All too often properties are admired, even studied, on the basis of their architecture, while the landscape component is marginalized. This tendency is furthered by the fact that good landscape design often does not call attention to itself. The results can seem elegant, fitting, and natural, but observers often do not think about how they got that way or who was responsible for that resolution. As in any field, recognition entails understanding, and here the challenge is formidable indeed. Since the 1970s enormous advances have been made in our knowledge of the history of twentieth-century landscape design in the United States, but much more needs to be done in scholarship and advocacy.

One way to foster the process is integration, that is, looking at architecture, landscape architecture, or, for that matter, planning not as discrete entities, but as part of a larger whole. Here the concept of landscape as J. B. Jackson advanced it, or cultural landscape as it is often called today, can serve our purposes well. Through this process, we can learn more as well as present a compelling case for preservation. A cultural-landscape approach certainly enriches the meaning of all the types mentioned thus far and of many others as well.[17] Dulles International Airport in Fairfax County, Virginia (1958-1962), is mostly presented in publications as a building, but it is really a system and a setting, without which the Saarinen terminal loses much of its meaning. While cast as a landscape design, Halprin's Freeway Park in Seattle (1976) derives much of its impact from a defiant relationship with the broader urban context—the canyons of skyscrapers that abut it and the cacophony of the sub-grade channel for motor traffic it temporarily mitigates.

The same can be said within the vernacular realm, which is of immense importance to understanding any era, but all too often receives little attention when it is still perceived to be new. Numerous community gardens of Washington, D.C., dating from World War II and later decades, for example, are of interest for the patterns of both individual and collective human activity they manifest, but take on added significance when they are understood as antidotes for the neatly ordered apartment dwellings, often with their own manicured landscapes, where many of the participants live (Figure 9).[18] Conversely the tended and sometimes secluded ambience of the motel landscape of the 1950s and 1960s

Figure 10. Motor House (Woodlands) motel, Williamsburg, Virginia, 1956; Department of Architecture, Colonial Williamsburg, architects and landscape architects; mostly demolished 2001 (Longstreth, 1997)

Figure 11. J. B. Jackson house, La Cienega, New Mexico, 1965; J. B. Jackson, designer (Longstreth, 1998)

Figure 12. Gettysburg National Military Park, Gettysburg, Pennsylvania, established as a federal battlefield park 1895 incorporating land developed by the Gettysburg Battlefield Memorial Association since the 1860s; general view showing former visitor center in background (Longstreth, 1999)

offered a sense of relief and relaxation after hours of driving through disorderly highway landscapes. Landscape can also be a manifesto, as at the Motor House, a motel complex created by Colonial Williamsburg, Inc. (1956), which stood in silent protest against the kind of laissez-faire strip development that was increasing exponentially in that community and nationwide (Figure 10).

From this perspective, landscape is greater than the sum of its parts, but without landscape design the whole cannot be comprehended. Imagine, for a minute, how anyone could attempt a serious discussion of J. B. Jackson's house near Santa Fe without addressing its landscape components in detail (Figure 11). How self-evident, we assume, because of the formative role Jackson had in such thinking as well as the extraordinary character of the scheme. It should be just as evident that a work by Richard Neutra such as the Kaufmann house in Palm Springs must be considered in the same terms, given his concern for, and knowledge of, landscape architecture, yet that integrative approach is almost never taken, at least in print, because of the architect's fame.[19] The intellectual baggage that must be shed in most cases is substantial. The political baggage of the preservation community may be even greater. The fracas that has been percolating in recent years over Gettysburg National Military Park gives ample evidence of the problem.

I use Gettysburg, which is not centered on landscape design per se, because I am struck with how quickly many landscape architects, their profession's press, and even a number of experts in the natural sciences grasp the issue at stake, while the architectural press does not seem to have a clue and the so-called national leadership of preservation cannot emerge from a banal "this-versus-that" argument.[20] At stake is the former visitor center of 1959–1961, designed by Richard Neutra and indeed a major work of his as well as the flagship of the Park Service's Mission 66

Program and one of the most sophisticated designs for a federal building realized during the postwar era.[21] The charge among the building's detractors is that it violates the hallowed battleground, even though the siting "right on the resource" was then a carefully developed Park Service strategy. Many preservationists take the side door out, as it were, stammering that, well, yes, the building is important, but it is not as important as the battle, and therefore . . . .

What all this dithering obfuscates is the fact that the building was conceived as an integral component of the park, not just in topographical terms, but in programmatic ones as well (Figure 12). Placement close to the scene of the decisive confrontation, Pickett's Charge, one of the bloodiest and most consequential military engagements ever fought on American soil, was meant to drive home a message at the height of the Cold War. Neutra conceived the project as a testimonial to Abraham Lincoln, to his Gettysburg Address, to American freedom, and most importantly to world peace. When the intent is understood, the building becomes more than an abstract composition "imposed" upon a pastoral landscape. It is at once a declarative and deferential part of that landscape, which is, of course, a complex, evolving commemorative landscape, one of the richest we have. The park superintendent's insistence that this gory section of the battlefield be "restored" is as intellectually preposterous as it is intellectually puerile, given the many later components that will remain and the phalanx of commercial establishments that lies conspicuously close by.

We cannot tolerate such either/or scenarios—history versus architecture, landscape versus architecture, or any such artificial divisions. They do an acute disservice to the past. An integrative approach, by contrast, can enrich our outlook and make the past both more accessible and engaging. Landscape architects and historians of landscape architecture, by the very nature of their work, are particularly well suited to taking a leading role in such efforts if they choose to do so. No field for such exploration is as fertile as the recent past, when even some of the most assertive new machines were tempered by the garden. The last landscape cannot become a thing we know only from memory.

Richard Longstreth is a professor of American Civilization and director of the graduate program in Historic Preservation at George Washington University, Washington, D.C. He has written extensively on historic preservation subjects pertaining to twentieth-century America. His publications include: The Mall in Washington, 1791–1991; The Drive-In, the Supermarket, and the Transformation of Commercial Space in Los Angeles, 1914–1941; *and* City Center to Regional Mall: Architecture, the Automobile, and Retailing in Los Angeles, 1920–1950, *winner of the Lewis Mumford Prize for Best Book Published in American City and Regional Planning History.*

NOTES

1 I chose "The Last Landscape" as the title of the paper from which this article was developed simply because it was an engaging and economical way to introduce the ideas developed below. Subsequently, I recalled that, of course, this was also the title of a once well-known book by William H. Whyte (Garden City, N.Y.: Doubleday, 1968), which advanced a much-praised, but largely-unheeded call for reform in the design of outlying portions of the metropolis. The fact that this book has been forgotten in many quarters only underscores the tenuous position of things from the recent past.

2 For background, see Richard Longstreth, *City Center to Regional Mall: Architecture, the Automobile, and Retailing in Los Angeles, 1920–1950* (Cambridge: The MIT Press, 1997), chap. X. Many writings pertinent to the subjects discussed in this paper are contained in Richard Longstreth, comp., "A Historical Bibliography of Architecture, Landscape Architecture, and Urbanism in the United States since World War II," posted on http://www.recentpast.org. Few historical writings exist on the subjects discussed in the text; most of the references cited represent a sampling of contemporary sources.

3 Sidney Nichols Shurcliff, *The Day It Rained Fish & Other Encounters of a Landscape Architect* (Gloucester, Massachusetts: The Pressroom, 1991), pp. 151ff. For contemporary accounts, see idem, "Shoppers' World: The Design and Construction of a Retail Shopping Center," *Landscape Architecture*, July 1952, 144–51; and Robert L. Zion, "The Landscape Architect and the Shopping Center," *Landscape Architecture*, October 1957, 6–12.

4 James S. Hornbeck, ed., *Stores and Shopping Centers* (New York: McGraw-Hill, 1962), pp. 131–38.

5 Louise A. Mozingo, "The corporate estate in the USA, 1954–64: 'Thoroughly modern in concept, but...down to earth and rugged'," *Studies in the History of Gardens & Designed Landscapes*, January-March 2000, 25–56; idem, "Campus, Estate, and Park: Lawn Culture Comes to the Corporation" in Chris Wilson and Paul Groth, eds., *Everyday America: Cultural Landscape Studies after J. B. Jackson* (Berkeley: University of California Press, 2003), pp. 255-74, 348–51.

6 "Rural Insurance Plant," *Architectural Forum*, September 1954, 104–107; "Insurance Sets a Pattern," *Architectural Forum*, September 1957, 113–27.

7 "John Deere's Sticks of Steel," *Architectural Forum*, July 1964, 77–85; "Bold and Direct, Using Metal in a Strong, Basic Way," *Architectural Record*, July 1964, 135–41; Donald Canty, "Evaluation: The Wonders and the Workings of Saarinen's Deere & Co. Headquarters," *AIA Journal*, August 1976, 18–21.

8 Scott Wilson, ed., *Hollin Hills, Community of Vision: A Semicentennial History 1949–1999* (Alexandria, Virginia: Civic Association of Hollin Hills, 2000; Mark A. Klopfer, "Theme and Variation at Hollin Hills: A Typological Investigation" in William S. Saunders, ed., *Daniel Urban Kiley: The Early Gardens* (New York: Princeton Architectural Press, 1999), pp. 47–64.

9 "Second-Home Communities," *Architectural Record*, November 1965, 152-55; "Ecological Architecture: Planning the Organic Environment," *Progressive Architecture*, May 1966, 120–35.

10 Barbara M. Kelly, *Expanding the Dream: Building and Rebuilding Levittown* (Albany: State University of New York Press, 1993); Cynthia L. Girling and Kenneth I. Helphand, *Yard Street Park: The Design of Suburban Open Space* (New York: John Wiley & Sons, 1994), chap. 4; Richard Longstreth, "The Extraordinary Postwar Suburb," *Forum Journal*, Fall 2000, 16–25.

11 "Fresno Downtown: Pedestrian Preserve," *Architect & Engineer*, March 1960, 12–13; "Heart of Gruen's Fresno Plan," *Progressive Architecture*, January 1965, 184–86; "Upgrading Downtown," *Architectural Record*, June 1965, 175–90; George W. Wickstead, "Critique: Fresno Mall's First 12 Months," *Landscape Architecture*, October 1965, 44–45, 48.

12 Joe Bower, "Kalamazoo Keeps Stalled Mall," *Preservation*, January-February 1997, 18–19. The mall was eventually retained, but redesigned.

13 Jane Jacobs, "New Heart for Baltimore," *Architectural Forum*, June 1958, 88–92; William H. Potts, Jr., "Charles Center in Baltimore: How the Plan Didn't Get Compromised," *Landscape Architecture*, January 1969, 122–27; "Hartford: Renewal in the Round," *Architectural Forum*, December 1960, 72–76; "Planning the Downtown Center," *Architectural Record*, March 1964, 178–87).

14 Although I did not realize it at the time the paper was prepared, work was under way on a historic district nomination for Lafayette Park, the initial portions of which were designed by Ludwig Mies van der Rohe, Ludwig Hilberseimer, and Alfred Cauldwell (1958–1962). As of November 2002, that nomination had been approved by the Detroit Historic Designation Advisory Board and was waiting approval by the City Council.

15 Frederick Gutheim and National Capital Planning Commission, *Worthy of the Nation: The History of Planning for the Nation's Capital* (Washington: Smithsonian Institution Press, 1977), pp. 313–23; Pamela Scott and Antoinette J. Lee, *Buildings of the District of Columbia* (New York: Oxford University Press, 1993), pp. 242–45.

16 Stephen J. Thompson, "Philadelphia Design Sweepstakes," *Architectural Forum*, December 1958, 94–99; Edmund N. Bacon, "Pei in the Sky and Other Aspects of the Philadelphia Story," *Architectural Association Journal*, November 1963, 103–12; Philip Herrera, "Philadelphia: How Far Can Renewal Go?" *Architectural Forum*, August-September 1964, 179–93; William L. Rafsky, "Success Comes to Society Hill," *Historic Preservation*, September–October 1966, 194–95.

17 The literature on cultural landscape is now, of course, extensive, and historians of the built environment have argued for a more integrative approach for some years; e.g., Dell Upton, "Architectural History or Landscape Architecture," *Journal of Architectural Education*, August 1991, 195–99. To my knowledge, however, the discussion of how landscape design can enrich a broader view of landscape history has been minimal.

18 Richard Longstreth, *History on the Line: Testimony in the Cause of Preservation* (Washington: National Park Service, and Ithaca, New York: National Council for Preservation Education, 1998), chap. V.

19 Concerning the Jackson house, see Marc Treib, "J. B. Jackson's Home Ground," *Landscape Architecture*, April-May 1988, 52–57. The importance of landscape for Neutra is evident in his presentation of the Kaufmann house, see W. Boesiger, ed., *Richard Neutra: Buildings and Projects* (Zurich: Editions Ginsburg, 1951), 70–79. See also Richard Neutra, *Mysteries & Realities of the Site* (Scarsdale, N.Y.: Morgan & Morgan, 1951).

20 John Beardsley, "Another Battle at Gettysburg," *Landscape Architecture*, September 2000, 128, 125. Compare with Allen Freeman, "Unwelcome Centers," *Preservation*, July–August 1997, 16–17; and Thomas Hine, "Which of All Pasts to Preserve?" *New York Times*, 21 February 1999, AR-48.

21 Sarah Allaback, *Mission 66 Visitor Centers: The History of a Building Type* (Washington: National Park Service, 2000), chap. 3. The most fully developed argument of the building's historical significance is contained in the National Historic Landmark nomination, prepared by myself and Christine Madrid French for the Society of Architectural Historians and summarily rejected by National Park Service officials, posted on http://www.recentpast.org.

This charter was drafted on the occasion of the Preserving Modern Landscape Architecture symposium held at Wave Hill and Columbia University in New York City on April 5-6, 2002.

We, the undersigned speakers and attendees of this national symposium, believe that the time has come for the American Society of Landscape Architects (ASLA) to develop national guidance and ethics regarding the ongoing preservation and management of nationally significant works of landscape architecture from the recent past. This critical period, from just after World War II until the Bicentennial in 1976, must be addressed before it is too late. To allow seminal works of landscape architecture to be destroyed or altered without any informed public discourse edits out a significant chapter in the evolution of our profession. Therefore, we, the undersigned, ask that the ASLA develop a stewardship ethos for addressing the documentation, treatment, and management of this unsung and highly vulnerable aspect of our profession's heritage.

Name (print)	Signature
STUART O. DAWSON	
Tina Bishop	
PHYLLIS ANDERSEN	
KEN SMITH	
Gregg Bleam	
Franco B. Lombard	FRANCES LOMBARD
CHARLES BIRNBAUM	
Jean Garbarini	
Chris M. Panos	
ARLEYN A LEVEE	
STEPHEN WING, ASLA	
KATHRYN WOLF	
LAURIE OLIN	

Name (print)	Signature
PATRICIA MC.DONNELL	Patricia McDonnell
MARK JOHNSON	M.
Laurie Matthews	Laurie matth
PATRICIA JONAS	Patricia Jonas
CRISTINA CASTEL-BRANCO	Cristina Castel-Branco
Elizabeth Barlow Rogers	EBRog
Janet Waterhouse	Janet Waterhouse
ROGER P. LANG	Roger P. Lang
MARC TREIB	Marc
Ed Bennis	EM Bennis
JESS CANFIELD	J. Canfield
MARGARET STORROW	Margaret Storrow.
JOHN KINSELLA	John Kinsella
Donald C. Richardson	Donald C. Richardson
P. A. Rolland	
MARTIN SKRELUNAS	M.
JoAnn Beck	JoAnn Beck
Tatyanna Seredin	
CAROLINE ROB ZALESKI	Caroline R. Zaleski
Shauna Gillies-Smith	Shauna Gillies-Smith
MICHAEL McCLELLAND	

PRESERVING MODERN LANDSCAPE ARCHITECTURE II

Name (print)	Signature
STEPHEN B. MOHR	*[signature]*
GAIL WITTWER-LAIRD	*[signature]*
GRANT JONES	Grant T. Jones
CHARLOTTE FRIEZE	Charlotte Frieze
JESSIE SNYDER	*[signature]*
Peter T. Kelly	Peter T. Kelly
ANDREW MOORE	*[signature]*
JENNIFER HARMON	*[signature]*
ANN GRANBERY	Ann Granbery
DIANE KANE	Diane Kane
ANNE RAVER	Anne Raver
ADRIAN SMITH	*[signature]*
ELIZABETH GRAFF	Elizabeth Graff
BARBARA S. OLEJNIK	Barbara S. Olejnik
DARWINA NEAL	Darwina L. Neal
RICHARD LONGSTRETH	*[signature]*
Heidi Hohmann	Heidi Hohmann
Paul Bennett	*[signature]*
[signature]	
MARY DANIELS	Mary Daniels
MARION PRESSLEY	Marion Pressley
Lucy Lawliss	*[signature]*